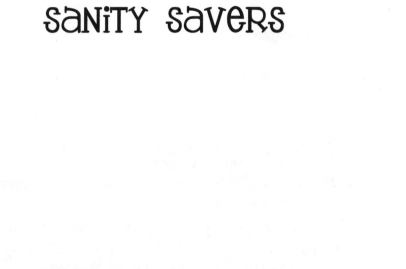

SANiTY SaVeRS

Dedication

Sanity Savers is dedicated to all the teachers I worked with over the years. We talked, laughed, and shared. They helped save my sanity with their encouragement and their generosity of heart.

Additional books by Sharon MacDonald

All About Community Helpers
All About Farms
All About Transportation
BAGS
Block Play
Everyday Discoveries
Idea Bags for the Kitchen: School-to-Home
Idea Bags: Activities to Promote the School-to-Home Connection
Jingle in My Pocket Book
Squish, Sort, Paint, and Build: Over 200 Easy Learning Center Activities
The Portfolio and its Use: A Road Map for Assessment
Watermelon Pie and Other Slices

SANITY SAVERS

FOR EARLY CHILDHOOD TEACHERS

200

Quick Fixes for Everything from Big Messes to Small Budgets

Sharon MacDonald

Illustrations by

Kathy Dobbs

gryphon
house®, inc.
Beltsville, MD 20704

Bulk purchase

Gryphon House books are available for special premiums and sales promotions as well as for fund-raising use. Special editions or book excerpts also can be created to specification. For details, contact the Director of Marketing at Gryphon House.

Disclaimer

Gryphon House, Inc. and the author cannot be held responsible for damage, mishap, or injury incurred during the use of or because of activities in this book. Appropriate and reasonable caution and adult supervision of children involved in activities and corresponding to the age and capability of each child involved, is recommended at all times. Do not leave children unattended at any time. Observe safety and caution at all times.

Every effort has been made to locate copyright and permission information.

Copyright

Published by Gryphon House, Inc.
10726 Tucker Street, Beltsville, MD 20705
301.595.9500; 301.595.0051 (fax); 800.638.0928

Visit us on the web at www.gryphonhouse.com

Library of Congress Cataloging in Publication Data

MacDonald, Sharon, 1942-
  Sanity savers for early childhood teachers : 200 quick fixes for everything from big messes to small budgets / by Sharon MacDonald ;
[illustrations by Kathy Dobbs].
     p. cm.
  Includes bibliographical references and index.

  ISBN13: 978-0-87659-236-6
  ISBN10: 0-87659-236-1

  1. Early childhood teachers--Job stress--United States. 2. Early childhood teachers--Time management--United States. 3. Early childhood
education--United States. I. Title.
  LB2840.2.M22 2004
  372.11--dc22

                              2004001109

SANITY SAVERS

TABLE OF CONTENTS

IDEAS FROM SHARON
I have learned that dealing with crayon marks, spills, and stains requires calmness. In the end, calmness cleans just about as well as most household cleaning products.

IDEAS FROM SHARON
Interruptions for emergencies in the classroom are quite another matter. Respond to those as you have been directed in your school district's guidelines.

TRY THIS!

Use leftover laminating film to keep glue and other spills from damaging tables and to protect easels from excess paint and gooey media. Laminating film is very slippery, so keep it off the floor. Protect floors in the easel area with shower curtain liners or oilcloth taped down.

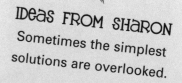

IDEAS FROM SHARON
Sometimes the simplest solutions are overlooked.

IDEAS FROM SHARON
Don't wait for the big closet of your dreams. Deal effectively with and be thankful for the storage space you have now.

TRY THIS!
Store materials for outdoor use near the door to the outside. You will be more willing and able to set up outside centers frequently.

IDEAS FROM SHARON
Children want to please the important adults in their lives. When they don't, it is mostly because they don't know how.

SANITY SAVERS

FYI:
Songs are like messages in a bottle. They carry skills and concepts to new places in the brain where information can be speedily retrieved.

INTRODUCTiON

Sanity Savers was written to help reduce some of the unnecessary stresses of your everyday classroom life. The solutions in this book are meant to give you more time to teach and allow you to enjoy your time with the children in your classroom.

The best way to use the table of contents or the index in this book is to find a subject that interests you and begin reading. There's no need to read the book from cover to cover. You'll find that the "Ideas From Sharon" and "Try This!" sections throughout broaden the discussion of a topic in interesting ways.

Many of the solutions in this book are as playful as the children you teach. It is important to have fun—to let young children play—because it is through play that children learn. It is the "tool" children bring to the cognitive exercise of learning.

I know that the ideas, tips, and solutions in this book work because I used them myself over the 28 years I taught. Looking back, I realize that the first few years of my teaching career were difficult because I had trouble organizing my classroom and managing children's behavior. Teaching is hard, and you learn along with the children.

IDEaS FROM SHaRON
Act calm. It is important to model this behavior. No one will notice if you are faking it.

Making things better in the classroom means anticipating problems and heading them off. The more experience you have with guiding young children through the days in your classroom, the better equipped you will be to stay one step ahead of the action. It will make life easier for you and leave you more time to teach.

Much of your success depends on how you introduce the children to the new experience of learning. I suggest that you focus on letting them know your expectations. This will help the children develop a routine that is beneficial to you and the success of the class. Many times I found that I did not know in specific terms what I wanted from them. Then, I was in trouble. How could they know what to do if I didn't know myself?

Teach the children your expectations and work on basic citizenship skills. It is the best way for children to learn to help themselves and each other with problems and frustrations, so that you can spend more time helping them to learn!

Many different circumstances can interfere with your ability to teach the children. One of these is inadequate space. In many settings, there simply is not enough space to have centers, materials, supplies, furniture, and of course, the children themselves, who function better with lots of "elbow" room.

Some challenges are about money. You must spend your own money on many things for the classroom. However, these additions will make your teaching more effective and your life easier.

There are challenges about time. There doesn't seem to be enough of it to plan, read, fill out forms, meet with peers and parents, deal with crises, create activities, and teach.

IDEAS FROM SHARON

A delightful book of lists by Judy Fujawa entitled *(Almost) Everything You Need to Know About Early Childhood Education* offers more ways to bring variety, interest, and new ideas into the classroom.

There are challenges with classroom management. Every classroom is as unique as the children in it, and teachers must identify the best ways to teach to fit the room as well as the class.

The interplay of the challenges of time, money, space, behavior, and exceptions make every classroom a unique and extraordinary test of your resourcefulness.

So how can you begin to make your teaching life easier?

Let's restore the expectation that teaching is fun, and focus on changing the environment rather than trying to change the children when things aren't going well. Let's take the time to let the children know how to use things and build in them the trust that the environment will support their explorations, offering many rich learning experiences. Be sure to take time to explain safety in situations involving heat, broken glass, and any other potentially dangerous activity. Do not use toxic materials around the children. Careful supervision should be used in all potentially dangerous situations. The best time to do this is the first four weeks of school. You can read more about it in Chapter 1, "The

4-Week 'Fix' That Lasts All Year." I suggest that you read it in short spurts so you can focus on the content. It is not a quick fix, but it is an essential one.

Most importantly, you must accept and enjoy the children. They have needs you must try to understand. They give teaching its meaning, and they invent your experiences faster than you can anticipate them.

I often think of my experiences in the classroom as a pile of stones 28 years high. Each time I reached in to grab a stone, the rest would shift toward the breach in the pile, as if to say, "Try me next." Maybe it will be the same with you. You, too, have your own pile of stones. In this book you'll find more to add to your pile to enrich the wonderful work of teaching children.

IDEAS FROM SHARON
With young children, building self-esteem is more important than imparting information.

SANITY SAVERS

The "4-Week 'Fix' That Lasts All Year" means taking the first four weeks of the school year to teach the children to be successful in your classroom. This is difficult because there are so many other demands on your time. During the first four weeks, however, if you take the time to teach the children in your classroom about how your classroom works, everyone will have a much easier time throughout the remainder of the year. Here is why. Children need to learn to function independently of you and to depend on themselves and their peers for help. The first four weeks is the time to start putting their independence into action.

Children will deal with peers as they grow into adults. Dealing well with others is an essential learned skill. We hear and read every day about how communities benefit from citizens working with each other to tear down the "fences" of misunderstanding.

These skills begin to develop when children share an environment with their peers. The classroom is where meeting personal needs requires meeting the needs of others. Learning to consider others is the first step in social learning. Beginning this way also relieves us of always being the one to help. Our job is to teach children how to learn, not to dispense information.

Chapter 1

THE 4-WEEK "FIX" THAT LASTS ALL YEAR

Be sure to take time to explain safety in situations involving heat, broken glass, and any other potentially dangerous activity. Do not use toxic materials around the children. Careful supervision should be used in all potentially dangerous situations.

The techniques discussed below have helped me introduce children to ways they can become more independent and increasingly self-reliant. These qualities emerge from everyday situations in the classroom. The following techniques are for use principally in center-based classrooms.

1. Introduce one center at a time during the first four weeks of school. Involve all of the children to generate the behavior guidelines for each center. Be sure to have extra transition time for cleanup, beginning and ending center activity, and for ending the day. The centers you have introduced to the children will run smoothly in the long run. It can be difficult, loud, confusing, and messy, but stay calm. Your work will pay off.

2. Be available for redirection throughout the classroom. This is called "accordion" teaching. This means that you will sit with a small group of children for 10-15 minutes, then get up and move around the room for about 5 minutes. This allows for redirecting, reminding, and reassuring the children. After you move around the room, sit with a different group of children, and continue this way until you have worked with all of the children.

3. Make sure your written and spoken directions are clear. Much of what is seen by the teacher as noncompliance is misunderstanding on the child's part. Give instructions orally and then have the child restate the instructions to you. Then, ask the child to model proper use of your directions. That child might easily become your new activity peer tutor (see page 85). Other children will often go to her for assistance.

4. Share your expectations. Tell the children what they will be doing and how they will work independently of you, either in small groups or alone. Explain why working independently is important.

5. Teach basic problem-solving skills. Children need to learn these to get what they need from others. The first step in problem solving is to arrive at some understanding and agreement of what the problem is. They start to ask the question "Why am I upset?" Putting a problem into words, or

at least trying, is a good beginning even if children can't quite express what they are feeling.

With help from the teacher in the early stages of this new awareness of themselves, the problem-solving process begins. In my experience, children's first steps are taken from the insight that, sometimes, a problem is not what it seems to them.

6. Teach the children to negotiate. They first learn about negotiating by doing it with you. You model behavior, and they emulate it. Negotiation starts with a statement of the problem. The child restates the problem. The secret to negotiating is being willing to let the other side get something they want so you can get something you want. Model negotiating, and you will gradually become the arbitrator. Resolution is eventually left to the children.

7. As arbitrator between two disagreeing children, offer several resolutions to a problem. For example:
   - Use a timer to measure how long a child works with mutually desired materials or equipment; other children have the same amount of time.
   - Teach them to be experts on their own behavior, not others' behavior. Use "I (feel)..." talk, not "You (are)..." talk.
   - Roll dice or flip a coin for indecision.
   - Make a waiting list (see page 34).
   - Work together on a project.
   - Take turns without timing the turn taken.
   - Play the "Rock, Paper, Scissors" game.
   - Use "Quiet Lotion" as "Problem-Solving Lotion" (see page 93).
   - Use a Complaint Book (see page 32).
   - Explain that everyone has an equal right to the same things.
   - Teach children to walk away to avoid worsening a problem.

IDEAS FROM SHARON
Emotions are natural. Accept children's moods and emotions as the best they can come up with at the moment. They will become less emotional as they learn and trust the classroom rules and that you will be fair with them. They will also learn that although they may have to wait, they will get a turn eventually.

IDEAS FROM SHARON
Smart Start by Pam Schiller is an excellent book on how to build brainpower in the early years. Chapter 9, "Problem Solving and the Brain," discusses problem solving and how it "is one of the brain's favorite exercises" and how "the brain only learns when confronted with a problem." It is important to remember that we need to let children come to their own solutions whenever possible.

8. Anticipate behavior problems and act before they erupt. For example:
   - Have clear boundaries for centers and activities.
   - Change center locations if conflicts occur.
   - Eliminate "runways." Runways are areas of the classroom that invite running. Usually, they are long, straight areas in the room. The traffic pattern works best when the areas of the room are arranged in a zigzag design rather than in long stretches of empty space.
   - Take time to be sure everyone knows how to work in a center and to use the activities properly.

IDEAS FROM SHARON

A book to use as an additional resource for how to use logical consequences, teacher language, and rule simplicity is *Rules in School* by Kathryn Brady, Mary Beth Forton, Deborah Porter, and Chip Wood, published by the Northeast Foundation for Children.

9. Use the "remind, redirect, and remove" sequence to modify young children's behavior. You will have to get directly involved, however, when safety is a concern and when you are serious about the children working independently. It is not necessary to say, "Stop," "No," or "Don't" unless the child's physical safety is in jeopardy. These words may buy you a little time but they just invite the opposite behavior. Also, if you use them frequently, children will ignore them. To review:

   - Remind the child how to use the activity.
   - Redirect the child when the reminder fails to change behavior. Demonstrate the correct use of the activity and then watch the child model the new behavior for you.
   - Remove the child if misuse continues and encourage her to choose another center. Tell her she can try it again tomorrow.

   Every day is a new day. Extending a consequence or saving a consequence until the next day is a day too late. Sending a note home is five hours too late. Consequences must be immediate if they are to be effective. Follow-through is essential to the children's learning.

10. Enact logical consequences for inappropriate behavior. Children need to know the consequences for their behavior. Make sure that consequences apply to what the child has done. Be even-handed.

Some examples of logical consequences:

- Break something? Put it back together, if possible.
- Knock something down? Help pick it back up or put it back the way it was.
- Spill something? Clean it up.
- Hurt someone? How about giving an ice pack or a cool towel?
- Knock down a building? Help rebuild it.
- Take away a toy? Give it back.
- Run around the room? Practice walking.
- Paint on someone's paper? Ask what you can do to make it better; try a little White Out on it.

11. Wait. Many problems resolve themselves. Frequent adult intervention in the solutions children devise is not wise. The resolution may not be "pretty," but move on.
    - Be calm.
    - Watch the action.
    - Walk toward the action.
    - Intervene only when safety is an issue or if you feel you must get involved. Remember that school is an important social learning place, not only for the children, but also for all the spectators. Remember how much you learned as a child on your own so you could fit in?

12. If a problem involves only an individual child, teach the child to use the "I Can Help Book" (see page 85), "Ask Three, Then Me" (see page 33), or to work with a Study Buddy (see page 33).

IDeas FROM SHaRON
Breathe deeply and often! Air is a natural tranquillizer and, if it is strong enough to hold up airplanes, it can sustain you.

THREE IDEAS ABOUT DISCIPLINE

1. Keep rules simple.

2. The logical consequence of a mistake is to correct it. An alternative often sought by teachers is to ask the child to say, "I'm sorry." It is difficult to pinpoint who is the offender in many situations. Children may feel that their teacher is taking sides. Also, insisting on an apology when a child does not mean it, or does not know what it means, is asking a child to misrepresent herself. That can hurt a child psychologically.

   Most young children aren't sorry in the same way that an adult feels sorry. Young children are not able to identify emotionally with others until they are farther down the developmental road, around ages 6-10.

3. Most children need to work off frustrations and release energy through outside play. The child that has the hardest time with the restrictions and rules of the classroom benefits most from outside play. Often, the teacher needs a break, too. Play can help.

IDEAS FROM SHARON
Act calm. It is important to model this behavior. No one will notice if you are faking it.

It is nice to let the children know what to expect in your classroom. It is like knowing that on the next page, you will find Chapter 2.

Teacher Resources

44 Routines That Make a Difference by the School Renaissance Institute

The ABCs of Quality Child Care by Aida Maria Clark

All Eyes Up Here! by Tee Carr

The Busy Classroom by Patty Claycomb

Life-Saving Strategies by Dottie Raymer

A Practical Guide to Quality Child Care by Pam Schiller and Patricia Carter Dyke

Skills for Preschool Teachers by Janice J. Beaty

A Survival Guide for the Preschool Teacher by Jean R. Feldman

Terrific Tips for Preschool Teachers by Barbara F. Backer

Cleanup is an essential part of the day, and can also be a fun teaching opportunity. Although cleaning up is often a source of conflict and power struggles, it does not have to be that way. It is important that the children learn to help, so make it more of a game and smile when you do it!

So, what's to teach? For one thing, cleanup teaches the children the importance of organization and structure. It also teaches the advantages of having an organized place to work. In addition, children learn skills such as matching, sorting, counting, observing, and comparing. With your help, they discover that cleaning up makes the day run smoothly, and order and organization make it possible to find what they need. This chapter offers clean-up solutions, clean-up tools, and clean-up strategies to use in your classroom.

Chapter 2
CLeaNUP

CLEAN-
UP
BAG

CLEAN-UP SOLUTIONS

No matter how tidy your room is, messes happen in the classroom. I have tried many different things over the years to find what works to clean them up. Knowing what to do made me feel less anxious about the seriousness of these semi-emergencies. The following solutions work.

Tempera Paint on Hard Flooring

Solution: Throw a ¼-inch-deep stack of unfolded newspaper on the spill. Let it sit for 5-10 minutes. Remove the newspaper. Allow the child who made the spill to use a large sponge to clean up what remains of the spill. If a child does not know how to rinse and squeeze a sponge, this would be a good time to teach him. The cleanup may require several rinses. If the stain persists, wait until the children leave for the day. Pour a little fingernail polish remover on the stain; wipe it up with a soft cloth.

Crayon Marks on Floor Tile, Plastic Surfaces, and Chalkboard

Solution: After the children have left for the day, spray a little WD-40 on the crayon mark and wipe it off with a soft cloth. Clean up what remains with a sponge and liquid detergent.

Cleaning Plastic Surfaces and Laminated Activities

Early in my teaching career I used moist paper towels for cleaning laminated and acetate materials. I put the towels in resealable plastic bags near the activities that required frequent cleaning. It didn't work. The towels would dry quickly, making them useless, or they would be too wet because the children would take them to the sink, wet them again, forget to squeeze them out, and drip across the floor. Splat! Water everywhere. What to do?

Solution: Keep flat, cotton cosmetic cleaning pads in three or four hinged-top, plastic soap dishes with a clip closure. Fill the soap dishes with the pads; add 15-20 drops of water and two to

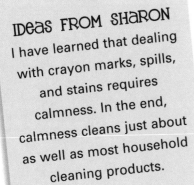

IDEAS FROM SHARON
I have learned that dealing with crayon marks, spills, and stains requires calmness. In the end, calmness cleans just about as well as most household cleaning products.

* Be sure to take time to explain safety in situations involving heat, broken glass, and any other potentially dangerous activity. Do not use toxic materials around the children. Careful supervision should be used in all potentially dangerous situations.

three drops of alcohol. The alcohol keeps the pads from souring. Close the soap dish and let them sit overnight. The pads will absorb the water and the alcohol. The children use the pads to wipe off marker lines, then throw the pads away. Pads work better than other wipes because they don't leave a

lanolin residue. Check the soap dishes often. The children may not tell you when they are empty, and you need time to prepare them since the pads have to absorb the moisture overnight.

💡 Dirty Hands

There are several ways to get paint, food coloring, permanent marker, and dirt off children's hands. Soap is always a good choice. Children love soap; they will lather themselves until the bubbles reach the ceiling. But soap won't clean much other than dirt. Children also have an interest in more "exotic" solutions. Here are a few.

Solution: Clean hands with a slice of raw potato. Children can stick their fingernails into the potato slice to get food coloring from under their nails. Lemon juice, vinegar, and hair spray work well, too. Place a small amount in the palm of one hand. If they're using lemon juice or vinegar they must rub briskly. If using hair spray, have them rub their hands with a rag. For really dirty hands use lemon juice and salt in a gooey paste. Ask them to rub their hands together for a minute or two and wash their hands afterward with soap and water.

💡 Marker Stains on Clothing

Solution: Put a paper towel underneath the stain. Pour on a little alcohol and blot the stain with a cotton ball. Change the paper towel as it absorbs the marker color. Advise the parents to wash the fabric with ¼-cup bleach and a color-safe laundry detergent.

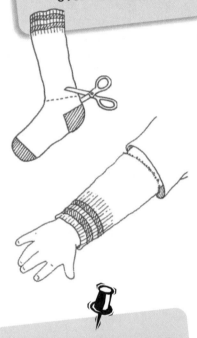
Tempera Paint on Clothes (except red and yellow)

It is frustrating for a child to get tempera paint on her clothes, especially when you have wrapped her from head to foot. And then you see it, one blob of paint on a little patch of exposed clothing you had not noticed!

Solution: One way to get the paint off is for you (not the children!) to spray the paint spot with 409 All-Purpose Cleaner, wait about a minute, and blot with a paper towel. Follow up with a drop or two of dishwashing liquid and water. Rub with a rag. Another method is to keep "travel packets" of stain remover pads on a shelf near the easel or art table. Follow the instructions on the packet. Travel or individual packets are costly, but are more convenient.

Getting red and yellow paint out of clothing is a different story. What you do depends on the kind of red and/or yellow that is in the clothes. Crayola.com has a number of suggestions for removing red and yellow paint (and other materials) from clothes. If either you or a parent is desperate for a solution, just hop online for some answers.

Gum in a Child's Hair

Solution: Put a little vegetable oil on a rag; rub gently. Or, if the child has no peanut allergies, you can use peanut butter the same way.

Clogged Sink

Waiting for maintenance or a janitor to unclog your sink often takes too long. What if you need the sink immediately because you've got some wet, gooey stuff that has no other place to go? Learn to attack it yourself. Here's how.

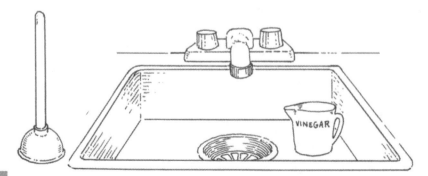

Solution: First, buy a plunger, label it as belonging to your classroom, and put it in a safe place where others will know that it is part of your materials. Put three Alka-Seltzer tablets down the drain; add a cup of white vinegar. Wait for 5 to 10 minutes. Turn on the hot water for a minute or two. If the water still stands, use the plunger.

🔆 Broken Glass

Broken glass is dangerous. The small pieces are hard to see and you're never sure if you have gotten all of them up. What to do besides sweep? Wipe!

Solution: First, be sure that all the children stay away from the area where there is broken glass and, if possible, move all nearby activities to other places in the room. Sweep up the area gently (just you, not the children) so that you don't disburse the shards beyond the area of breakage. Wet three or four paper towel sheets and wipe up the small slivers of glass from all surfaces. Repeat one to two more times. If you have a vacuum cleaner, use it last.

TRY THiS!
Clean glass, mirrors, and windows with Glass Wax (available in the floor wax section at many hardware and grocery stores) to protect them from grubby hands and unknown drops and splashes. It makes the glass easier to clean.

CLEaN-UP TOOLS FOR CHiLDReN

Children can help you clean up the room, especially after activities. Make them part of cleanup every day. Collect tools and supplies that are easy for the children to use. Make a permanent place for the clean-up tools, a place children can go to every day without having to ask you. Following are some tried-and-true suggestions for clean-up tools.

🔆 Sponge

Cut a slit along the short side of a large sponge. Put a sliver of soap inside. Moisten the sponge and put it in a small clean-up bucket. The children remove the sponge, clean up an area, and return it to the bucket. The sponge re-soaps itself continuously.

Commercial-Size Bucket and Mop

Purchase a bucket and large, cotton-string mop. Before bringing it to the classroom, saw off 24 inches of the handle (to make it easier for the children to use). Sand the jagged edge smooth to remove splinters. Each morning, dampen the mop and put it in the mop bucket. The damp mop is too heavy for the children to pick up (which they would love to do), so what they can do is tip over the bucket, pull out the mop, and clean up a messy area. The children can replace the mop in the tipped-over bucket, and then place the bucket upright. It might take two of the children to upright the bucket, but they become very good at doing it—a task, by the way, that improves their gross motor coordination.

Liquid Trash Bucket

It has always been surprising to me how wet things can get on a child's short walk to the sink. Activities that require the disposal of liquid need a bucket. A plastic milk jug works well. Cut off the top quarter of the jug. Label it "Liquid Trash." Put it near the messy activity. The children pour their liquid trash into the bucket rather than walk across the room to the sink.

TRY THIS!
If a child has a splinter with about half of it exposed, Scotch tape will often pull out the splinter. Gently press a small piece of tape on the splinter and remove the tape.

Broom

Purchase an adult-size broom and dustpan. Before bringing it to the classroom, saw 24 inches off the handle. Sand the jagged edges smooth to remove splinters. Use this broom for big sweeping jobs. The small whiskbroom and dustpan work well for the small ones. Children can work in pairs on these jobs. They learn the Three "Cs" of working together while pushing the broom: Collaboration, Coordination, and Cooperation.

Clean-Up Tool Buckets

Gather two or three one-gallon ice cream buckets. In each bucket, put a small whiskbroom and dustpan, a magnet, a dry rag, two or three short socks or cut-off tube socks, and a brown paper lunch bag. Children use the magnet to quickly gather up metal objects that have fallen to the floor. The children put on the socks to clean up small spills and then throw them away. The paper lunch bag is for "lost" things (write "Important Pieces" on it). When the children find something of value on the floor, such as a puzzle piece, game piece, or letter of the alphabet, it goes in the bag. At the end of each day, go through the bag. You'll be amazed at what you find.

CLEAN-UP STRATEGIES:
Getting the Children Involved

Children need to feel that the classroom is theirs to enjoy, but they also must learn to help keep things clean and neat. The classroom is their community. You may ask them to pitch in to clean up an area they may not have played in. Some will resist. You must persevere. Pride and a sense of ownership are learned behaviors. We can begin to instill these virtues, resulting in an easier clean-up time. Here are some strategies to help you.

■ **Strategy 1:** Ask the children to clean up with your back turned to them. See if they can clean up "on tiptoes" without your hearing a sound.

■ **Strategy 2:** Use a 3-minute sand "hourglass" timer. The timer fascinates the children. One or two will often stand and watch it as sand falls from the top to the bottom. Give them a few minutes and then send them off to clean up.

■ **Strategy 3:** Time the children with a stopwatch. Make sure they know you are doing it. Ask the children to predict how long it will take to clean up the room. Set a kitchen timer for that length of time. When they have finished, compare their predictions with the actual results.

- **Strategy 4:** Stage a "cleanup race" between two teams. Who can finish first? This is noisy but effective if you don't use it too often, and the children really enjoy the race!

- **Strategy 5:** Clean up by crawling, sitting, kneeling, squatting, and standing. Ask them to change positions as they work.

- **Strategy 6:** Use a colorful, gift-wrap paper clean-up bag. Place two to three objects from each center in the bag. Write "Clean-Up Bag" on the front. Ask the children to reach into the bag, select an object, and put it beside the bag. They clean the center from which the object came. When they have finished, they return and remove a second object from the bag, and replace the first object into the bag. The children continue until the entire room is clean.

- **Strategy 7:** Make Clean-Up Cards. Before the children arrive in your clean classroom, take several pictures of it from several angles. During the first few weeks of school take photographs of the children cleaning up different centers properly.

Make Clean-Up Cards by gluing one or two photographs on cardstock. The photograph(s) show a child cleaning up a center or show the center clean and neat. A child may or may not be in the photograph. The class leader for the day deals

CLEAN-UP BAG

IDEAS FROM SHARON
The logical consequence of a child not doing his or her part is the loss of choice. Children respond well to having choices. They also respond well to gentle reminders, respect, and kindness.

out the cards to each child. A child gets a card and cleans the center in the photograph. The child returns the card when done, gets a new one, and cleans the next center until the whole room is clean. You will need about 40-50 cards because the children get new cards as they return the ones they already picked, and you won't run out if they return them quickly.

■ **Strategy 8**: Make a sign: "Loiterers will be put to work!" Hold it up when you see children who pretend to clean up while visiting with others or playing. Use this humorous strategy to help children learn that you will assign them a task if they don't contribute to the clean-up effort on their own.

■ **Strategy 9**: Clean-up caps and aprons: Get each child a baseball cap or an apron. You can find these at discount stores. When it is clean-up time, have them put on their hat or apron to become the classroom "Clean-Up Service." You can even make aprons from dishtowels (see page 102).

■ **Strategy 10**: Ask the children to sign up on a "Sign-Up Sheet" for the space they want to clean. Younger children will need help with this. Also, many children may want to clean up the same area. Have a plan to deal with this when it happens. You can limit the number of spaces available on each sign-up sheet, or ask the children to clean up in groups of three or four.

■ **Strategy 11**: Clean up to music. Without a song, cleanup may seem to drag on. Use the children's favorite songs, but change them frequently. A good one is "Jump Down, Turn Around" (available on many CDs for children). I adapted the lyrics of this song to whatever we were cleaning up in the classroom. For example:

Jump down, turn around, and pick up the games.
Jump down, turn around, and put the games away.
Everybody's working to pick up the games.
Everybody's working to put the games away.

Work standing up! Work sitting down!
Work on your knees with the games all around!
Work standing up! Work sitting down!
Putting the games away.
—by Sharon MacDonald

IDeas FROM SHARON

■ Brain research has shown that singing releases endorphins in the brain that encourage children to think more positively about themselves and the activities that they may not like to do, such as cleaning up.

■ It is good to sing, no matter how well you think you can. The children will always enjoy singing with you.

HELPFUL CLEAN-UP HINTS!

Here are some ideas to help organize your room for easier cleanup:

- When you reorganize your classroom centers, take photographs before the children come to school. Put them on the Home Center cabinets and furniture to show where things go, like clean-up tools, dishes, glasses, dolls, and clothes.
- Place silhouettes on the Block Center shelves for the children to match blocks to their silhouettes as the blocks are put away.
- Create one special place for as many objects as possible. That way, there is less confusion as to what goes where and clutter is better controlled.

Cleaning up is a part of daily life, and the children can share the responsibility and take great pride in the results.

So, what's next? Interruptions. How you handle interruptions will help children learn that if they are going to get along in this life, they must make a place for others.

Teacher Resources

Hints From Heloise by Heloise

Teacher-Made Materials That Really Teach by Judy Herr and
Yvonne Libby Larson

Chapter 3

INTERRUPTIONS

Getting the attention of a group of young children is no easy task, and it is even more difficult to regain the attention of the group after an interruption. While teachers need to let children know that they cannot deal with interruptions constantly throughout the day, they also need to meet the challenge of preserving children's self-esteem and addressing important needs. It is hard to find the right balance. On one hand, young children are vulnerable and teachers want to help them. On the other hand, children require an introduction to patience, flexibility, and tolerance of the needs of others.

Early childhood teachers need to encourage children to find their own solutions and use other resources that are available to them, such as their peers. They can benefit from their peers' experiences. Other children have a remarkable ability to understand their peers' dilemmas and predicaments and to resolve them fairly. They are honest yet empathic to many circumstances their peers may face.

Interruptions detract from the value and coherence of what you teach. Some strategies for positively influencing behavior are discussed below. Vary your approaches so the children don't become accustomed to just one.

Complaint Book

May 8, 2004   2:00 PM

person making complaint _Katie_

event _Jacob would not share his crayons._

2 possible solutions

_____

_____

_____

Complaint Book

May 8, 2004   2:00 PM

person making complaint _Katie_

event _Jacob would not share his crayons._

2 possible solutions

_____

_____

_____

Complaint Book

Designate a notebook in which the children can "write" their complaints. Explain that adults often fill out a complaint form in a store if they are unhappy with something. Tell them they can write their complaints in the complaint book, just like their parents might do at the grocery store. The children do this on their own using real or invented writing and spelling. Ask them to include the date and time of the complaint, their name, a description of the event, and two suggestions of possible solutions.

Write the instructions above on the inside cover of the Complaint Book. Be aware of who is writing in the Complaint Book. With practice, it will be in your peripheral vision most of the time during the first six to eight weeks of the school year. That way, you'll know who wrote the entries that you are unable to read. If you notice a child writing in the book, you will know who to talk to about her "complaint."

Work one-on-one with the child to help her generate solutions to the problem. If you are teaching a small group, for example, and you notice a child writing in the Complaint Book, when it is possible, take the child aside and say, "Tell me about what you wrote in the Complaint Book." Discuss the problem and propose two solutions. You might say to the child, "When this happens again, try the first solution we talked about. See if it works."

Later on, go back to the child and ask if the first solution worked. If not, put the second solution in play. If necessary, repeat your discussions with the child to generate two new solutions if the first two do not work.

One outcome of using the Complaint Book in my classroom was that the children got tired of discussing problems and trying the solutions generated through the book. They felt they had more important things to do! They began to solve their own problems without writing in the Complaint Book.

Pay close attention to the Complaint Book during the first six to eight weeks of school. Soon the children won't be writing in it as much and what they do write is more significant. Using the Complaint Book moves the children toward the goal of solving many of their own problems, using the skills they have acquired by problem solving on their own and by watching how other children interact successfully. Often, the child solves the problem herself, and moves on.

"Ask Three, Then Me" and Study Buddies

My classroom experience led me to question how I could respond to the pleas for immediate help that came from the four corners of the classroom. Children can solve problems, too, I thought. Two useful approaches emerged: "Ask Three, Then Me" and "Study Buddy."

"Ask Three, Then Me" is a rule that required a child to seek the help of three other children before she came to me for help.

The child who is asked to help becomes a "Study Buddy." Select study buddies by putting all of the children's names on jumbo craft sticks. Select pairs each Monday morning. Be thoughtful about whom you pair so that the children work well together.

If a child has a problem that cannot be resolved by either of these approaches, help the child when you are free. Encourage the child to set the problem aside until you can help.

Stop-and-Go Hat

Purchase two baseball caps, one green and one red. When you are "open" for interruptions and questions, put on the green cap. Put on the red cap when you are "closed" for business. When the red cap is on, it means no interruptions.

An alternative to the Stop-and-Go Hat is a sign on a hat that says "go" on the front and "stop" on the back. Turn the hat forward when you are in the help mode, turn the hat backward when you are not.

IDEAS FROM SHARON
Keep children dispersed throughout the classroom by having one popular activity in each center. Dispersing the children keeps conflict to a minimum. Some children will find they are interested in the less popular activities after trying them.

Open and Closed Sign

Another way to influence the children's behavior is with a freestanding sign. The sign's front says "Open," and the back says "Closed." When you are open to give help, turn the sign outward toward the class. When you are occupied, show the "Closed" sign toward the class. The children know that now is not the time to ask for help. Be sure you are "open" for the majority of the day!

If a child ignores the signs and comes to you anyway, say, "Now is not a good time. Please see if a friend can help you. I will help you when I am free." If the child's behavior continues, ignore it until you are free. It is important that early in the school year, children learn that you mean what you say.
Follow through with what you tell the children and your class will run smoothly.

Waiting List

A popular activity is like a magnet—all the children want to get there at once. The solution is to make a waiting list on a clipboard. Number the lines and encourage the children to sign up for their turn. When a child finishes, she draws a line through her name and calls the next person on the list. Waiting lists decrease interruptions, and reduce the number of times you hear children arguing. The waiting list also keeps children from hanging around to get a turn, so conflict is reduced or eliminated. Children can use invented spelling and writing. You will be amazed at how quickly young children learn to read each other's names, even if the spelling and writing is invented. If this doesn't work, you can give the children laminated name or picture cards to put on the list.

Library Center
1. ~~Tommy~~
2. ~~Cassandra~~
3. Kathleen
Tomorrow
1. Benjie
2. Mark
3. Alix

"Talk to Me" Face

Take a portrait picture of yourself with a digital camera. Ask another teacher to help if you have trouble taking it yourself. Enlarge the photograph; glue it to a jumbo craft stick. Write the words, "Talk to me!" at the bottom of the picture. When you are not available, put the face in a place clearly visible to the children. Have the children talk to the picture when they cannot talk to you. The children understand that this is just a fun, temporary solution, but it might help them solve problems themselves by talking about them.

Picture Directions

Picture (rebus) directions are great at reducing interruptions. Teach the children to use them. Draw step-by-step directions to instruct a child through an activity without outside help. This allows children to be more independent when doing an activity. Four examples follow.

Using the Thermometer

warm water   ice water

1. Put the thermometer in the warm water.

   What happened?

2. Put the thermometer in the ice water.

   What happened?

Snowball Printing

You need:

yarn balls

paper

divided tray with paint

1. Dip the Snowball in the paint.

Name

Name

2. Print on the paper with the snowball.

Ice Melting

1. Put the ice in a pan.

2. Wait 1 hour.

3. Look at the ice.

What do you see?

SANITY SAVERS

Winter Word Box

Winter Words

snow

Choose a winter word and try to write it.

💡 Tape Recording

When children in your class have a problem and you can't help right away, ask them to tape record the problems and include in the recording how they would like to resolve them. You can listen to the recordings with each child afterward and discuss solutions. Sometimes, just recording the problem relieves the child's frustration.

💡 Fill a Bag With Troubles

Have a stack of brown paper lunch bags next to the trash can. When a child is frustrated, encourage her to fill the bag with her troubles, crumple it, and throw it away.

Trouble Trash Can

No one can escape occasional interruptions, but you can minimize them if you put some of these strategies in place. What's next? Saving money. So, pick up your wallet and turn the page. Let's go shopping!

Teacher Resources

Challenging Behavior in Young Children: Understanding, Preventing, and Responding Effectively by Barbara Kaiser
Conflict Resolution Activities That Work! by Kathleen M. Hollenbeck
Fresh Approaches to Working With Problematic Behavior by Adele M. Brodkin
Kindness Curriculum by Judith Anne Rice

SANITY SAVERS

Teachers are always looking for ways to save money. Few teachers have enough money to buy essential materials and supplies, especially with tight budgets and so many classroom needs. Saving money is especially important to first- and second-year teachers who, being new to the profession, are exploring ways to save money while buying essential materials for their classrooms. Using inexpensive materials helps teachers save money for special items and spend less money out-of-pocket.

The ideas in this chapter focus on 10 inexpensive, common classroom materials. For each material there are several ideas for using the material in creative ways. While you are no doubt familiar with the materials, you may not have thought of using them as suggested.

The 10 materials discussed in this chapter are: adding-machine tape, jumbo craft sticks, leftover laminating film, toilet paper cylinders, clipboards, muffin tins, clear-plastic shoe bags, plastic milk jugs and lids, film canisters, and placemats. You can find these and other affordable classroom items at garage sales, dollar stores, party stores, office supply stores, and school supply stores.

Chapter 4

Saving Money

Ideas from Sharon
Experienced teachers tend to find a simple material that works and stick with it.

ADDING-MACHINE TAPE

Adding-machine tape on rolls is an essential item for the classroom. Buy a package of 24 rolls of 3-inch-wide adding-machine tape. It should last all year. Try these activities using adding-machine tape.

IDEAS FROM SHARON
Long stories written by older children on adding machine tapes are fun "secret writings scrolls."

All About Me

Give each child a roll of tape and a rubber band to use during the year. Store all the rolls in one basket. The children use the adding-machine tape to write stories on. Older children write such things as: I have ____ eyes. I have a dog named _____. I like to eat _____. I live at _____. They could also write or draw about something they saw or learned that day.

After each child has used his tape, he rolls it up and secures it with a rubber band, then returns it to the basket. Place each roll in a resealable plastic bag labeled with the child's name.

Headbands

Use the tape to make headbands to dramatize stories. Glue photocopies of animals or story characters on the headbands. Size the headbands to each child and tape the ends together. The children put on the headbands to dramatize characters from stories and plays. If children dramatize what they are learning, they retain the information more easily than reading or hearing it.

☀ Timeline

Make a timeline to keep track of the number of days (or hours, minutes, or attempts) that it takes to complete a project, and keep track of changes that occurred, or use it to record events.

☀ Measuring

Use adding-machine tape as a non-standard measuring device. Children can measure each other's height, for instance, or the circumference of a ball, or the width of a table. When they tear off the tape or cut it with blunt-end plastic scissors, they can compare the lengths.

When children are able to answer the question, "Which is longer, wider, or taller?" they can then use standard measurements, such as inches and feet, to measure the non-standard unit they have taken with the adding-machine tape. Moving from non-standard to standard measurement increases the difficulty of a measurement activity. You can modify activities with adding-machine tape by changing the task you ask a child to do. Operating a classroom in this open-ended way reduces the money you have to spend to meet the diverse ability levels of the children in your classroom. You can challenge older children, while meeting the developmental levels of younger ones.

JUMBO CRAFT STICKS

Craft sticks are reasonably priced and easy to find. Start the year with three boxes of 1000—this is usually enough to last all year. Here are some things you can do with them.

☀ Study Buddies

A study buddy is another child to whom a child with a problem goes for help. Put each child's name on a jumbo craft stick. Put the sticks in an orange juice can covered with aluminum foil. Each Monday, select pairs of children to be study buddies for the week. The following week, mix up the sticks and do it again.

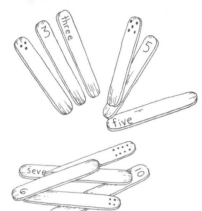

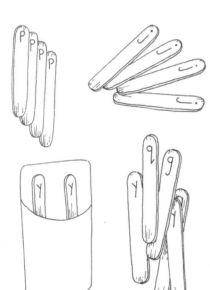

Alphabet Match

Write the 26 letters of the alphabet in upper- and lowercase on craft sticks. Have the children match the upper- and lowercase letters.

Number Match

On one set of craft sticks, write numerals that you want to teach, for example, 1 to 10. On a second set of sticks, write the corresponding number words you want to teach, for example, one to ten. On a third set of sticks, make dots that correspond to the numbers and words you have written on the other two sets of sticks. The children match the numbers on the first set of sticks to number words on the second set and then to the dots on the third set. For example, the child would match 6 to six to :::, and so on. Use colors to create self-correcting sets. For example, 6, six, and ::: would all be written in red.

Hang-Down Letter Sort

Write the five lowercase "hang-down" letters "p," "j," "g," "q," and "y" on four sets of craft sticks. You will have 20 sticks. Ask the children to match them in groups of four. Teaching these in a group can help children learn that these five letters are the only ones in the alphabet that hang below the base line.

Money Sticks

Enlarge actual coins on the copying machine to make photocopies of money for the sticks (dollar bill, quarter, nickel, dime, and penny). Enlarge them to a size that will be easy for all the children in the group to see. Glue each image to a craft stick and make enough for each child in the class to have one. When the children are learning to identify coins, have the children hold up the correct sticks as you name the coins. If the children are working on making change, ask one child with a nickel to stand up and then ask five children with pennies to stand up. Talk about how one nickel is worth the same as five pennies.

💡 Story Word Sticks

Write the key words for each story or topic on craft sticks. Key words are words you want the children to remember and learn. They have topic or story significance and they are readily built from the children's experiences in everyday life. Put the sticks for each story in an orange juice can covered with aluminum foil. If you are doing a story, as opposed to a topic, label a can, "The Three Little Pigs." Each of the sticks would be labeled with one of the words, "pig," "wolf," "hay," "twigs," and "bricks." If you are studying apples, for example, label the can "Apples" and write "apple," "seeds," "apple tree," "applesauce," "apple pie," "apple juice," and "core" on the craft sticks.

IDEAS FROM SHARON
Any image on a stick can become a puppet!

TRY THIS!
Children can hold craft sticks under print to guide them as they read.

💡 Color Sticks

Make color sticks to use as a substitute for liquid food coloring. It is easier to use food coloring in this way, and it limits the amount used. Buy Wilton Icing Colors in small foil-topped jars of red, yellow, and blue. Cut a slit the width of the craft stick in the aluminum foil seal. Push a craft stick through the foil about one inch, and as you pull out the stick the excess food coloring paste is wiped from the stick. Wipe off the excess color icing paste with a paper towel.

Push the craft sticks color end up into a block of Styrofoam. It will take about a week for the color to dry. Wipe the sticks every other day with a paper towel to remove a little of the coloring. This will help the coloring dry without being sticky to the touch. This might take up to a week in a humid climate and just a few days in dry locales. When the sticks are dry, store them in a plastic resealable bag. Use the color sticks as you would use food coloring. Color sticks last for years. Moisture activates the color stored in the craft stick.

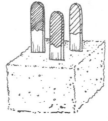

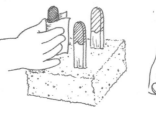

Step 1   **Step 2**   **Step 3**   **Step 4**   **Step 5**

Craft Stick Puzzles

Draw puzzles on jumbo craft sticks. First, tape a few sticks together side to side with masking tape, and then draw a picture on the other side. When you take the tape off, the children can put the sticks together like a puzzle.

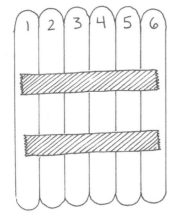
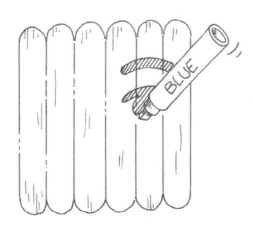

LEFTOVER LAMINATING FILM

Throwing away leftover laminating film frustrated me, so I started experimenting with ways to reuse it. It was worth the effort! I tried to get as much as I could by using what no one else wanted. To collect leftovers, I put a box with my name on it next to the laminating machine at school. I spread the word that I wanted leftovers and asked all the teachers and assistants to fill the box. They did. Give the collection box a try, and try the ideas below with the laminating film you collect.

Laminating Film Art

In the Art area, draw with permanent markers on laminating film and hang it in the windows. The effects are spectacular.

Winter Streamer

Make a winter streamer. Use 3' strips of laminating film and coat hangers. Cut the strips into 2 to 2 ½" widths. Shape the coat hanger into a circle; tape the ends of the streamers around the coat hanger. Make a handle from the coat hanger hook by squeezing it closed with pliers and taping around it with masking tape. When the streamers are ready, turn on the music and have the children take turns doing a winter dance.

Transparent Things Finger Hunt

Save the small cuttings of laminating film. If you have larger pieces, cut them into smaller ones. Dump them all in the water table. You will need lots of cuttings! Don't add water, as it would be difficult to clean up.

Place other transparent objects among the cuttings, such as film canisters, small plastic bottles, bottle caps, buttons, plastic shoe buckles, pipettes, barrettes, rubber worms, shower curtain rings, banana hairclips, and food wrappers. Select items that are safe for the children to find among the cuttings (i.e., no pointed objects or objects with sharp edges).

This activity invites young children to refine their developing fine-motor skills by feeling for the objects below the surface of the cuttings. They learn the approximate characteristics of things and make guesses about shapes. Their brains form mental images of the objects they find before the objects become the actual physical structures they see when they pull the objects from the table. This is good stuff for young brains! Before a child peeks, ask him to guess what's in his hand.

Block Center Windows

Invite the children to use the laminating film to make "windows" in the Block area. Put the laminating sheets in a basket along with a roll of tape. The children tape the film to the small openings in their block structures.

The next two ideas using laminating film require large sheets, not small scraps, of laminating film.

See-Through Reading Folders

Use laminating film to make see-through reading and writing folders that stick to the edges of the printed pages. The children can use them during reading time to write on the laminating film with overhead marking pens. The laminated panel sits over the print. They can copy letters, shapes, and words, or underline or circle words and refer to other writing elements depending on the topic you are teaching.

Cut two identical rectangles of laminating film just a little larger than the book pages you want to overlay. Lay the film pieces side by side about ⅛" apart. Run a strip of masking tape between the panels, holding the panels together, and then fold on the masking tape seam. To use, hold the laminated panels with the taped side on the right. Slip the printed page between the panels. Children can circle words, shapes, and story characters; underline letters or words; and circle punctuation. They wipe off their writing with cleansing pads from a soap dish (see pages 22-23).

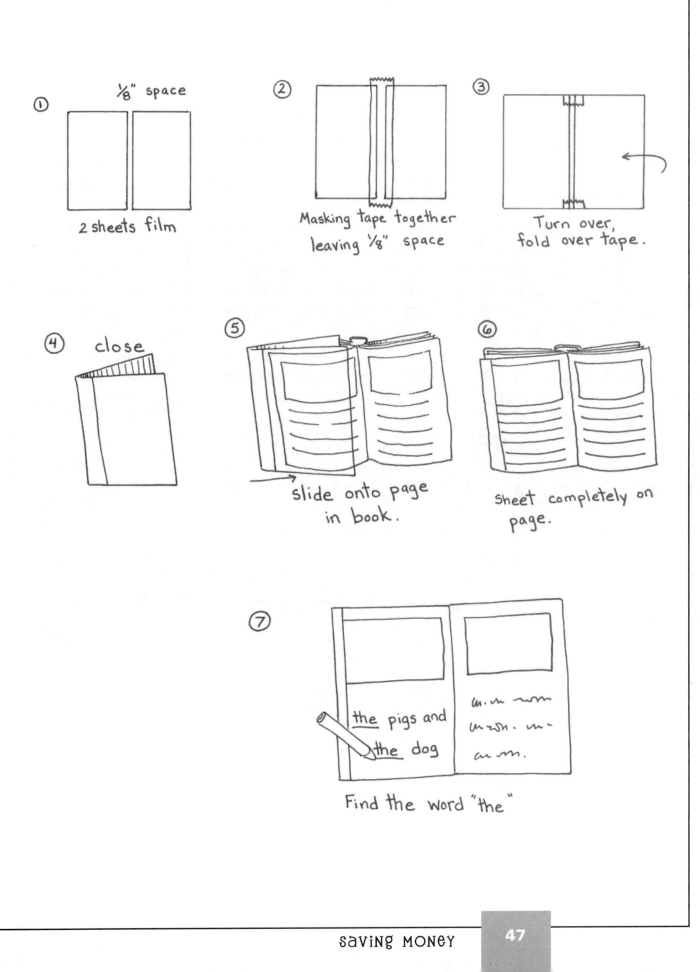

① ⅛" space

2 sheets film

② Masking tape together leaving ⅛" space

③ Turn over, fold over tape.

④ close

⑤ slide onto page in book.

⑥ sheet completely on page.

⑦ the pigs and the dog

Find the word "the"

☀ Write-On Big Book Panels

Make large, transparent write-on panels to use with big books. This can be done in two ways:

■ Purchase acetate sheets (which is like laminating film, but stiffer). Use a clothespin to clip one sheet over the page the children are reading. They can write on the panel, underline words, and find specific words in the text using an overhead marker. Each page can be used 12-15 times, and then thrown away.

■ Cut poster board to the size of a page of a big book. Cut a rectangle out of the center to create a frame with about 2 ½" on each side. Cut a large piece of laminating film slightly smaller than the outside edge of the frame and tape the film to the backside of the frame. Use the laminated frame to clothespin over the page in the big book you want the children to use. When they are finished, they wipe off their writing with cleansing pads from a soap dish (see pages 22-23).

TRY THIS!
Use leftover laminating film to keep glue and other spills from damaging tables and to protect easels from excess paint and gooey media. Laminating film is very slippery, so keep it off the floor. Protect floors in the easel area with shower curtain liners or oilcloth that is taped down.

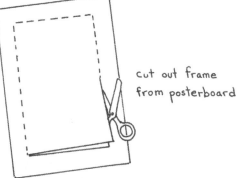

cut out frame from posterboard

tape film on back of frame

Big Book

SANITY SAVERS

TOILET PAPER CYLINDERS

Toilet paper cylinders are a very easy material to acquire. Ask the children's parents for contributions! You will always have a large supply. Here are a number of ways to use them:

Wind Sock

Cut 1–1½" x 12" streamers from tissue paper, or buy rolls of decorative streamers. Glue the streamers around the circumference of one end of the cylinder and let the streamers hang off the other end. Use a hole punch to make two holes in opposite sides of the top, tie a 24" length of string through both holes, tie the string ends together, and hang the windsock from a tree. Watch the wind blow!

Number and Letter Game

Cut the cylinders into 1"-wide sections. Let the children paint some of the sections red and others yellow. Use stick-on letters to put consonants on the red rings and vowels on the yellow ones. Cut 12" to 24" lengths of yarn. Challenge the children to make words by sliding the letters on the lengths of yarn. You can also use the cylinder sections with numbers. Put numbers, dots, and number words on the sections. The children can: (1) put the numbers in order 1 to 10; (2) match the numerals to the number words, (3) match the numerals to the number of dots, and (4) match all three. For example, ask them to match 8 with eight, 8 with ::::, and 8 with :::: and eight.

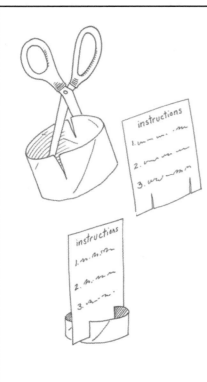

💡 Circle Art

Cut the cylinders in half. Have several colors of tempera paint nearby in small trays. The children dip the open end of the cylinders in paint and print with them on paper.

💡 Instruction, Picture, and Card Stand

Cut the cylinders into thirds to make three 2" rings from each cylinder. Cut two slits in the edge of a ring, opposite each other, about one inch deep. Cut two slits in the bottom edge of what you want to stand up (for example, an index card with picture directions). Match the slits on the ring. The slits will interlock when you slip the slits on the card into the slits on the ring and push them together. When joined, the index card edge and the ring will sit flush on the table. If you want to display a larger card, picture, or instruction, use two stands.

CLIPBOARDS

Clipboards are an inexpensive way to manage your classroom and keep things organized. You can purchase inexpensive clipboards if desired, or you can make your own using two clothespins and stiff cardboard. A major advantage to making your own is that most manufactured clipboards have a hole in the clip. The children love to put their fingers in the hole, which often results a semi-emergency when a child gets his finger stuck. Teachers love finding ways to avoid situations like this one. Often, it is the simpler, inexpensive approach that works best with young children.

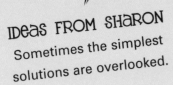

IDEAS FROM SHARON
Sometimes the simplest solutions are overlooked.

Here are some ways to use clipboards to manage your classroom:

Sign-in

When children choose an area, have them sign in when they enter. This provides a record of where each child played, which can be useful at clean-up time. If a child says, "But I didn't play there..." you have a signature to assign responsibility for clean up. Younger children may need assistance with signing in on the clipboard.

Waiting List

Sign up at a favorite activity. Use a waiting list that is no longer than the number of children who can actually do the activity that day (usually no more than three names, sometimes just two names).

Supply List

Keep a clipboard on a cup hook beside the door and keep a running list of supplies needed for the classroom. Have the children write what is needed on the list. With the list by the door you'll remember to look at it as you go out.

Portable Tabletop

Use a clipboard to write on when there is no table or desk around. You may find this useful when sitting on the carpet in a group, or outside.

"Must Do" List

Have a clipboard handy to keep a running list of things that need to be done. Model this for the children and they will follow your lead. Encourage them to add to their lists when things that need to be done occur to them.

> **Ideas from Sharon**
> Why have no more than three names on the waiting list? Because if all the children on the list cannot do the activity that day, the unfulfilled child often will not be very happy. It is better that you start a new list for the next day than have an unhappy child who could not be "squeezed in" to the schedule today.

MUFFIN TiNS

Your friends and family most likely have muffin tins somewhere around the house that are waiting to be transformed into something extraordinarily useful for the classroom. Ask for donations!

Art Materials Container

Muffin tins are great for holding collage materials for art projects.

Paint Container

Line muffin tins with aluminum foil cupcake liners to hold tempera paint to make less mess.

Juice Serving Tray

Use muffin tins to carry small cups of juice for snack. You can ask the children to help pass out the juice without fear of overturned cups.

Texture Match Game

Use muffin tins to make a texture match game. Glue a variety of different-textured items to the bottom of each cup section. Have matching textured pieces in a small basket nearby; the children match textures.

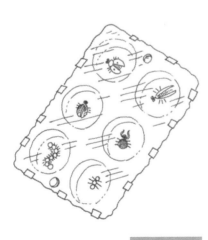

Observation Tray

In the bottom of each muffin tin section, glue things you want the children to observe but not touch (for example, dead insects with all of their parts still intact). Cover the entire tray with two layers of clear plastic wrap and tape tightly around and under the muffin tin.

Color-Mixing, Water-Watching Tray

Have the children use a pipette to move water, colored with food coloring, from cup to cup on the muffin tin. Use primary colors in three of the sections. When the children move the water, they mix the colors, too.

Magnet Work

This magnet activity works best using a microwave-safe plastic muffin tray. Collect a number of items that are attracted by a magnet, such as paper clips, metal filings, small washers, nuts, and bolts, as well as other materials that aren't attracted by a magnet, like sawdust, cloth, paper, and plastic. Put each of the materials in a section of the plastic muffin tray. Cut a sheet of laminating film to cover all the sections of the tray. Tape the film securely over the tray top. The children test each material to see which material the magnet will attract.

Note: Check periodically to be sure the laminating film is still firmly attached to the tray.

PLASTIC, TRANSPARENT SHOE-STORAGE BAGS

Shoe-storage bags are usually made for household use and hung on the inside of a closet door to keep shoes off the floor. They often are made of transparent plastic or cloth and can be purchased inexpensively at discount stores (they tend to be more expensive in specialty travel shops). The bags are more costly than most things you will buy for your classroom, but they are worth the investment. Here are just a few ways to use transparent shoe-storage bags.

Woodworking Tools

Use the bag to store tools for the Woodworking Center.

💡 Clean-Up Tools

Hang one in your classroom closet to organize all your cleaning supplies and equipment.

Safety Note: Make sure to keep this closet door locked at all times so the children cannot reach toxic cleaning products.

💡 Art Supplies and Instruments

Store art supplies and small musical instruments in the individual compartments.

💡 Home Center Shoe Storage

Store shoes in the Home Center.

💡 Teacher Tools

Store your supplies—a stapler, a roll of tape, paperclips (in a small, resealable plastic bag), pencils, pens, a staple remover, a hand-held pencil sharpener, Sharpie pens, an extra stamp pad, Band-Aids, and glue—in one place.

💡 Outbox

Hang a shoe bag on the classroom door as an "outbox." Label the compartments for each child and put messages, notes, and reminders there. As the children exit for the day, they pick up what needs to go home. The biggest benefit is that it serves as a reminder for you! Use the top row of the rack, out of the reach of the children, for things that you need to take home.

PLaSTiC MiLK JuGS aND LiDS

Milk jugs are easy to find and easy for parents to contribute. Ask for the jugs and the lids. Here are some ways to use jugs and lids.

Water Plants

Watering plants during vacations is impossible unless you can entice someone on the school staff to do it for you. Coming back to sick plants after a vacation is not a great way to start a new week. Here is a solution that worked for me.

Fill a plastic milk jug with water. Set the jug on the floor or on a stand so that the water level in the jug and the top of the pot are level. Use a length of cotton cord (available from your local fabric shop). Put one end of the cord in the jug; wrap the other end around the base of your plant. The cord works like a wick: the water "walks" right up the cord, continuously watering your plant. It works for about one week.

Funnel, Tube, and Container

Use milk jugs for outside water play. The illustrations on the next page show how to cut a jug in half to make a funnel from the top and a container from the bottom. Cut off the handle of another jug to make a short tube or "hose" and throw the rest of the jug away. Be sure to cut the jugs smoothly and sand any rough edges. The children enjoy watching water travel through the tube. They scoop up water, pour into the

TRY THiS!
If you lose Bingo discs that children use to cover the called number, letter, shape, or color during a Bingo game, use milk-jug lids instead.

iDeAS FROM SHARON
Transparent toys and objects are great for young children. They like to see inside things to find out what's going on, which is why lots of young children try to take things apart. Mechanical toys with transparent outer "shells" are ideal. Transparent piggy banks, for example, are good for saving coins. The children get to see the coins lying in the bottom, and then watch them shifting positions when they shake the piggy bank.

funnel or hose, and watch it fall into the container. Having transparent cups, buckets, tubes, and bowls offers the children many opportunities to learn by watching water move.

Beanbag Toss

Cut off the top one-third of five milk jugs. Write the numbers 1–5 on the jugs. Place them in a row. Make a throwing line by taping masking tape to the floor. The children stand behind the line to throw. To make a beanbag, fill a tube sock with beans and tie the tube (upper portion of the sock) in a knot. The children toss the beanbags at the jugs and add up their points. It is a great way to get them to work with numbers and add the points they earn. Improvised addition, on a grand scale, is to be expected.

Lid Sorting Tray

Glue the milk lids to a cardboard sheet in any pattern you want. The children sort dissimilar small objects into the lids and use one-to-one correspondence (for example, by putting one marble, one washer, or one bolt in each lid).

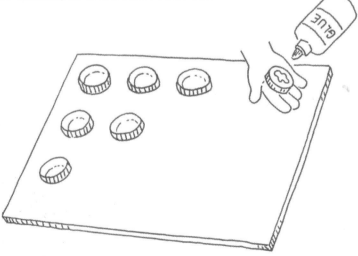

IDEAS FROM SHARON

A good source of ideas for toys that can be made from ordinary materials is a book series by Linda G. Miller and Mary Jo Gibbs, *Making Toys for Infants and Toddlers*, *Making Toys for Preschool Children*, and *Making Toys for School-Age Children*.

WASHED FILM CANISTERS AND SPICE BOTTLES

Film canisters and empty, plastic spice bottles can be obtained easily and washed so they can be used in the classroom. The use of digital cameras means that there are fewer film canisters around but try asking the people who develop your film to save them for you. Both containers save you money. Here's how.

Peanut Butter and Jelly

Use thoroughly washed containers to hold peanut butter and jelly. The children can make their own peanut butter and jelly sandwich using their own containers of spreads. They love to have individual servings of things. Making their own sandwiches helps build self-reliance and gives you a little extra time to do other things.

Smell Match

Make a "match the smell" activity. Make two containers for each scent. Use cotton balls in the containers with orange, lemon, strawberry, or chocolate flavorings and garlic, perfume, and cinnamon. Make holes in the container tops. In this activity, ask the children to match the smells.

When the containers are not in use, replace the lids. The smell will be retained for a number of weeks. If a smell weakens measurably, partially re-saturate the cotton ball.

Sound Match

Place a few small objects, such as buttons, small pebbles or gravel, paper clips, beads, and coins into the film canisters and close the lids. Make two containers for each object. The children try to match pairs of sounds by shaking the containers. Be sure to show the children the objects in each container before you set out the activity. That way, the children will be less inclined to open the containers to see what is inside.

> **TRY THIS!**
>
> You can use scrap pieces of lumber for a variety of activities, so keep some pieces at school and at home. A 12" long, 2" x 4" is useful as a surface for making holes in things, like film canisters and pill bottle tops—you make holes in the 2" x 4" rather than in counter tops and furniture, as I did for years. If you add a 16-penny nail and a 16-ounce hammer to your tool kit you'll be ready for almost any hole-making task. Ask the employees at your local hardware or home-improvement store for scrap pieces of lumber. Most of the time, they will gladly give them to you—especially if you identify yourself as a teacher of young children.

Canister Stringing

Collect film canisters. Throw out the tops and cut off the bottoms. Cut yarn in 36-inch lengths and have the children string the canisters on the yarn. Stringing builds fine motor and patterning skills and hand-eye coordination.

Cut off bottom of canister...throw away the top.

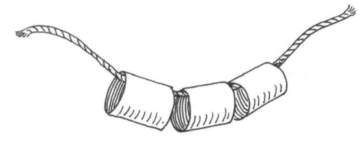

Glitter Shakers

Use the film containers to make glitter shakers. Fill the containers with all of your leftover glitter. The children draw designs on paper with glue and shake the glitter onto the glue. To make the shakers, use a hammer and a 16-penny nail to make five holes in the lids. Use a discarded piece of 2" x 4" lumber about 10-12 inches long for blocking.

School-to-Home Mini Tote

Use the containers to transfer important things from school to home, such as a baby tooth lost at school or other small items that might get lost in the transit home.

PLACEMATS

There are many designs and material choices to choose from but vinyl placemats hold up best. Here are some novel ways to use them.

Activity Mat

Define a child's workspace on a table or floor with a placemat. Put all the activity materials in a box or basket and put the box on the placemat. Materials stay on the placemat with the activity and hands stay at their work. If working on the floor with an activity, have one placemat for the child to sit on and one to define the workspace.

TRY THIS!
You can make two laminated surfaces stick together back-to-back if you first rough up the surface areas you want to glue together with sandpaper and then apply glue. This works if you are trying to glue a laminated pocket onto a laminated poster, for example.

Water Ponds

Use blue placemats to make ponds in the Block Center; add boats for use on the ponds.

Puzzles

Buy placemats of various appropriate shapes, such as animals, storybook characters, and pets. Usually, you can find vinyl placemats for most of the topics you study in your classroom. For younger children, purchase two identical mats and cut one into puzzle pieces; use the other for a puzzle base. The children assemble the puzzle over the base since it is easier to see how the pieces fit together. *(continued on the next page)*

For older children, cut only one vinyl placemat into puzzle pieces. Let them assemble it without a base to help them. Working a puzzle in this way challenges older children.

💡 Sewing Placemats

Sewing placemats helps develop fine motor skills. Purchase an interesting placemat and make holes around the edge about two inches apart. Use a hole punch. Purchase 72-inch-long shoestrings and have the children "sew" around the placemat edge.

💡 Count-Off Placemats

Write the numbers "1" through "10" on 10 placemats (one number on each). Ask each child to hold a placemat, and line up in numerical order (children need to learn that "1" is before "2"). They can help each other by talking about which number comes next. Ask the children to stand on the placemats after they have put themselves in numerical order. When called upon to do it, other children can gather in groups to match the number of dots on a card in their hands. This activity, or a variation of it, is an especially good activity for the child having difficulty recognizing numbers.

💡 Alphabet Mat

Ask the children to help you complete an "alphabet mat." Use an overhead marker (the ink washes off easily) on a vinyl placemat. Starting at the top left corner of the mat, write the lowercase letters "a" and "b" and skip two letters and the positions they would take up on the mat (the children will write the letters "c" and "d" in those spaces). The teacher then writes the lowercase letters "e" and "f," and again skips two letter positions (the children write the letters "g" and "h" in the spaces), then continues around the edge of the mat in this way to complete the alphabet.

SANiTY SAVERS

A second and more advanced option for this activity is to put a small basket of uppercase or die-cut letters in the center of the Alphabet Mat. The children match the uppercase letters to their lowercase letters written around the edge of the placemat.

Sink Safety Mat

Cut a hole the size of the sink drain in the center of the mat. When children wash dishes and other toys or materials in the sink, the placemat helps prevent slipping and breaking of items.

That's probably more than you wanted to know about doing things on the cheap. It is nice to use things twice and to use them for a new purpose. We have a lot to put away now. Where to put it? Turn to the next chapter and find out.

Teacher Resources

Making Toys for Infants and Toddlers by Linda G. Miller and Mary Jo Gibbs

Making Toys for Preschool Children by Linda G. Miller and Mary Jo Gibbs

Making Toys for School-Age Children by Linda G. Miller and Mary Jo Gibbs

Teacher Made Materials That Really Teach by Judy Herr and Yvonne Libby Larson

So now that you have all this stuff, where do you put it? And, a few weeks later, the question is surely, "Where did I put it?"

Storing and finding are twins who play well together but struggle when they are apart. What to do? In my early days of teaching, I always thought about box labels after I had put everything away, which was too late. Label things before you put them away.

CONTAINERS FOR STORAGE

You will have to box, bag, hang, and find all of your materials yourself. And, you will have to toss it out. It is hard to throw things away, especially when you have spent so much of your personal time making them. If you have not used something over the past year, however, the odds of you using it again are really quite small. Try some of the following ideas for saving space and storage.

Copier Boxes

Save copier paper boxes and store materials inside by topic or by center. Label the front, side, or box top with a detailed list of the stuff inside. Take a few minutes when you put materials inside to detail the box contents. It will save you hours of searching later. An important characteristic of any good storage box is a removable lid.

Plastic Tubs

Use plastic tubs for storage. It is a costly approach, but well worth it. Put all the materials in large 2-3 gallon resealable plastic bags and store the bags in plastic tubs. Tape a list of the contents to the inside of the lid.

Clear Plastic Boxes With Lids

Use under-the-bed, clear plastic boxes with removable lids. They are great for storing art materials, books, dramatic play props, and blocks.

⚡ Cut-and-Tape Charts and Posters

Cut oversize charts into thirds. Tape together with clear tape, and fold into standard-size storage boxes.

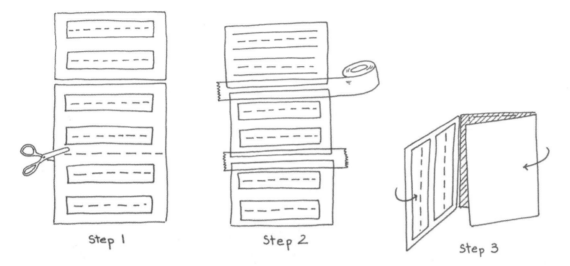

Step 1   Step 2   Step 3

⚡ Architectural Mailing Tubes

Store posters in architectural mailing tubes. Roll them with the front side out so they will roll against the wall and stay up when you tack them, rather than roll away from the wall and fall. Write the tube contents on a label on the outside of the tube.

⚡ Old Suitcases

Use old suitcases for storage. You can buy them at reasonable prices at flea markets, garage sales, and thrift or second-hand stores. Select suitcases without wheels and with old-fashioned latches.

IDEAS FROM SHARON

Old suitcases with old-fashioned latches and without wheels are the best ones to use. They are more childproof. If the suitcases have wheels, the children will roll them all over the classroom, and newer, simpler latches are easier for little hands to pop open. Store your materials in the suitcase and tape a description of the contents to the outside of the suitcase. Use the suitcase as a divider between centers and activities or store it under a table.

Clothes Hamper

A clothes hamper on wheels is a useful classroom addition, especially when you are changing activities and removing toys and equipment.

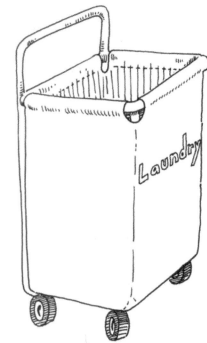

Brown Paper Grocery Bags

Store unbreakable things in brown paper grocery bags. Fill the bag, write the contents on the front, and store the bag in a tub or on a shelf.

Bags Made of Heavy Netting

Purchase several bags made with heavy netting. Tie them securely and hang them from bicycle hooks placed in the closet ceiling.

Miscellaneous Ideas:

Use any of the following for interactive charts, graphs, and poster storage:

- Artist's portfolio or chart boxes
- Pocket chart stand, clothes hangers, and clothespins
- Over-the-door hangers (typically used for clothes) with clothespins
- Skirt hangers
- Extra-large (poster size) resealable plastic bags
- Bicycle hooks on a wall or door to hold charts on notebook rings

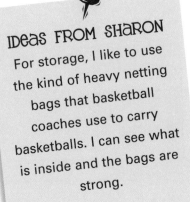

IDEAS FROM SHARON
For storage, I like to use the kind of heavy netting bags that basketball coaches use to carry basketballs. I can see what is inside and the bags are strong.

IDEAS FROM SHARON
If it is no longer useful, throw it away! You will always accumulate more over time.

SANITY SAVERS

WHERE TO STORE

So now that you have things labeled, boxed, bagged, hung, packed in tubs and in suitcases, where can you put them?

Storage at Home:

- Garage not used for car
- Ceiling of garage with car
- Underneath a bed
- In a closet where shoes were
- Underneath a table
- In a basement
- In an outside storage shed (be sure it is bug- and vermin-free)

Storage at School:

- In your closet (however small)
- Under against-the-wall tables
- As dividers between centers
- On a bookshelf used to rotate activities in and out of a nearby center

TRY THIS!

To conceal an area of the bookshelf you are using for storage, attach hook-side Velcro along the outer top, sides, and bottom of the shelves you are using. Cut a sheet of soft-side Velcro to fit the space. Apply the soft side to the hook-side Velcro, concealing what is on the shelf. You can purchase soft side Velcro by the sheet at fabric stores or from auto shops that do car interiors and install headliners. It is also available through school-supply catalogs.

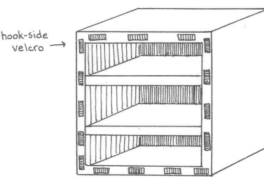

hook-side velcro →

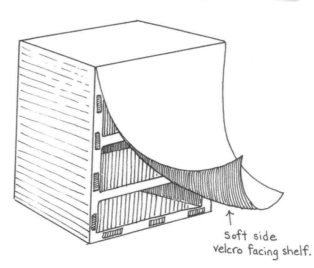

soft side velcro facing shelf.

You can also store thin boxes of materials behind a bookshelf, up against the wall. Turn an under-the-bed box sideways so it sits between the wall and the bookshelf. Above all, Go through your supplies regularly and get rid of things you don't use. Every time you take down a box, go through it. Label what you find on the outside of the box.

The next chapter is about making centers work in small rooms. It takes courage to take on a small room, along with everything else, but you can do it if you have a plan. Turn the page and take a look.

Teacher Resources

Creating Rooms of Wonder by Carol Seefeldt
Designs for Living and Learning by Deb Curtis and Margie Carter
Early Learning Environments That Work by Rebecca Isbell and Betty Exelby
Wonderful Rooms Where Children Bloom by Jean Feldman

If you find yourself in a small room that seems much too small, don't let it keep you from setting up a center-based classroom. It can be done. This chapter will help show you how.

Small rooms invite your creativity and will require lots of improvisation. In a small room, a filing cabinet drawer becomes a learning center, for instance. A plastic sweater bag can serve as a portable center that moves from one side of the classroom to another.

Chapter 6

SMALL ROOMS

In small rooms it is more important than ever to teach children how to use the materials in the classroom and respect the work and the "space" of others. The best time to do this is the first month of school. You will find the information you need in Chapter 1, "The 4-Week 'Fix' That Lasts All Year," pages 15-20.

Determine the movement of the children to and from centers and through the classroom before you set up the room. To minimize possible collisions, most activities need to be on a wall or on tables against a wall.

Managing children's behavior has become an especially important subject in the current school environment and is especially relevant to teachers in small rooms. Children come with different backgrounds, abilities, and developmental levels. Let's talk briefly about an overall strategy for dealing with behavior.

Managing behavior while maintaining self-esteem is a challenge for any teacher. The centerpiece of any approach is the absence of power struggles. Power struggles shift the balance of power from you to the child. For example, if you ask a child to do a classroom task and he does not do it, one solution is to walk away with the remark, "I know you can do it." Another solution is to give the child a choice such as, "Would you like to do it now or after snack?"

The two suggestions above assume that a child is not in physical danger. If a child is in danger, either remove the danger or remove the child.

Playing Outside

To help with space limitations, set up some centers outside. Most often, there is a lot more room out there! Creating outdoor centers replicates the cozy feeling of a room, a feeling that some children like more than others. Coziness can also be a source of behavior problems for some children who feel less "pressed" outside. Ask yourself, "What centers work best outside?" Here are some suggestions for an outside Art Center: an easel, chalk for sidewalk art and drawing, and big paintbrushes and a water bucket for "painting" fences and the sides of buildings. Other interesting outdoor centers include a Construction Center with boxes and hollow wooden blocks, a Games Center with a beanbag toss area, and a Library Center with a book nook in a small wading pool.

There are wonderful sources for outside play activities (see the list on page 119). Many include gross motor activities to use outside or in a large room, such as a small gym converted for such activities especially during the winter or on rainy days.

Let the children help you design outside play centers and move the materials in and out. Getting them involved from the start enhances their sense of ownership of the outside center. They will also take care of it more conscientiously.

If you have an assistant, divide the class in half. Let the assistant work outside with half of the class while you work inside with the rest.

With challenging children and difficult situations, use the time and energy you have to work toward the goal of self-management, not control. Children learn to manage their own behavior because good behavior is praised and bad behavior is not. Praise what you can through encouragement; ignore much of the rest. Be positive!

There are ways to set up the physical space in a small room for success, even if the room you're using seems unsuitable, such as a room that has large tables or mostly bulletin boards and windows, or one that has to be shared with another class and in which everything must be moved every day. Here are some ways to overcome these challenges.

Combine and rotate your centers every six weeks. Have the Library Center with a writing component all the time. Use this rotation scheme:

- Combine the Math and Science Center.
- Rotate Blocks with the Construction Center (e.g., Legos, Bristle Blocks, Tinker Toys) or Woodworking.
- Rotate the Art Center with the Music Center.
- Rotate Home Living with Creative Dramatics.
- Combine Woodworking with Writing.
- Combine Games and Puzzles with the Interactive Chart Center.

Small rooms require fewer centers at the same time, but you can still have all the centers in play at some point during the year. Here are some novel ways to resolve these unique problems: Use the backs of doors, the sides of filing cabinets, bulletin boards, and windows for center activities.

The following pages contain ideas about how to survive in a small room. They will make your room seem larger and your day seem shorter.

TRY THiS!
Retail stores that carry tubs and containers are all over the country. They often have resealable plastic bags in a number of sizes. Wait for a sale and buy a bunch. You won't regret it.

IDeas FROM SHaRON
Attitude and perspective make almost anything doable. The children notice and they model your behavior.

💡 Six-Pack-Ring Hanger

Tie six-pack rings together to make an activity center. Attach three to five rings across, and six to eight down. Tie them off as shown in the illustration. Weave them onto a shower curtain rod or a curtain rod. Make them as large as a small blanket or as small as a six-pack. Small ones can hang on a pants hanger (from the dry cleaners). Remove the cardboard cylinder from the hanger, slip on the rings, put the cylinder back on the hanger, and hot glue the cylinder at both ends. Hang this activity center at child height.

Put the activities in resealable, plastic bags and attach the bags to the rings with clothespins. The rings may sag under the weight of the activity in a bag, but as soon as the activity is removed, the rings return to its original shape. Six-pack rings hardly ever "die," so they make sturdy holders.

A six-pack-ring hanger can be used for storage as well as for a center. Make a large hanger on a curtain rod and hang the rod from a fishing line against a wall (so it won't move). Use the top half of the hanger for storage (that's the half the children cannot reach). Use the bottom for center activities that the children are actively using. Store all the activities in resealable, plastic bags and put the ones you aren't using at the moment high up on the hanger so the children cannot reach them.

TRY THIS!
Store activities in resealable plastic bags or small boxes so that all of the pieces can be kept together. An activity is not useable without all of the "moving parts."

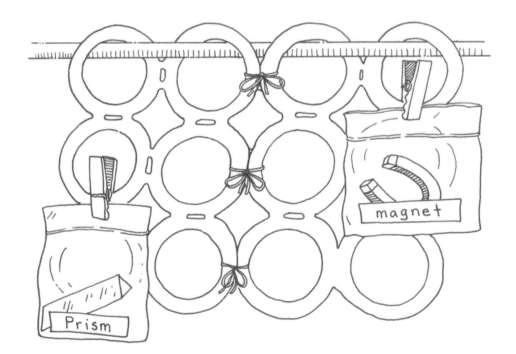

SANITY SAVERS

Large Tubs

Tubs require more of an up-front expenditure than you might feel comfortable with, but they are worth it, especially when you share a room with another teacher. Purchase 3′ x 2′ x 2′ stackable tubs with removable lids. Put your activities in two-gallon, or larger, resealable plastic bags and store the activities in the tubs. Label the outside of the tub with the center name and a detailed list of the contents. Stackable tubs are easier to access and put away quickly. They work especially well if you have large tables on which center activities can be laid out.

Hanging Sweater-Storage Bag

Sweater-storage bags usually come with a double hanger. They will hang flush with the wall and they have a long vertical row of lightweight shelves that are the perfect size for storing activities. Each shelf is usually six inches high and 12 inches deep. The bag may have a zippered front. Put activities in resealable plastic bags or small boxes, and stack them on the shelves of the bag. Display the bags with the zipper open (if there is one) and hang the bottom half of the bag at children's eye level. Use the top of the bag for storage and the bottom half for activities in current use in centers.

Lingerie Bag

A lingerie bag comes with a hanger, too. It is flat with a plastic, see-through front. It has about six different-size zippered pockets. They are great for small activities. Put an activity in each pocket and leave the pockets unzipped. Hang the bag at a child's height: low enough for most of the children to see into each pocket and have easy access to the pockets. Put each activity in a resealable plastic bag.

Shoe-Storage Bags

A discussion of shoe-storage bags is in Chapter 4, "Saving Money" (pages 39-61). Take a look. They are excellent money savers over the long run and they make wonderful centers for small objects and activities.

💡 Display Boards

Look in school supply stores for freestanding, three-panel, fold-out display boards made of colorful cardboard. The boards are 48" x 18". They are available in a number of colors—change colors with each center activity. Cut them in half horizontally with a mat knife; they will be 48" x 9" finished. Cutting the boards down makes them a good size for children in centers. Put the center activities in baskets next to the display boards. Display non-movable parts of an activity on a board (or explain and display some component of the finished activity). The boards take up little space and you can move them around easily.

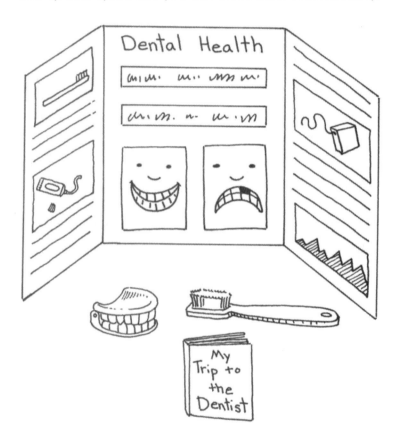

💡 Netting

Buy large pieces of orange safety fence and use it as netting. Orange safety fencing looks like large-gauge fishing net. Safety fence is used at construction sites to restrict access to unsafe areas. Hang the "netting" on a curtain rod against a wall. Attach objects to the netting and use it like a giant six-pack ring hanger (see page 72). It is made of plastic and it comes in two-, three-, and four-foot heights. It is available at hardware stores or home improvement stores. The netting is strong and durable and it

lends itself to storing heavy items like a bead-stringing activity in jumbo, resealable bags. The netting is also useful for hanging large buckets of heavier objects, like wooden puzzles and toys. Use clothespins and twist ties to attach objects to the netting. Attach the larger buckets with string, or clothespin the wire handle.

Ice Cream Buckets

Store things in the large ice-cream buckets from ice cream parlors. They may take up lots of space, but they are great to put activities in. Use ¾" bolts and nuts to attach them side-by-side (use three bolts to attach a container-pair). Attaching them together in this way allows you to pick up and reposition the whole unit, or to move it to a new location. They work great in room-sharing situations where you may have to pick up and move on short notice. They hold lots of activities because they are deep and sturdy. Use them both as an area divider and as storage devices.

Sides and Drawers of Filing Cabinets

Don't ignore the sides of the filing cabinets in your classroom. Magnetize your activities! Many games that might otherwise have to be put in a basket can be mounted on magnetic strips and stored on the bare sides of a filing cabinet.

Filing cabinet drawers are great to use as centers. If you have a four-drawer unit, use the bottom two drawers to put the center in. Put one center in front of the drawer divider, and put the second behind the divider. Use the top half of the filing cabinet for regular storage. Use two-drawer units for center storage exclusively.

TRY THIS!
Ice-cream buckets are specially made to hold up well and resist moisture. They are hard to get, but a local ice cream store might be able to help you (especially if you identify yourself as a teacher of young ice cream eaters).

IDEAS FROM SHARON
If you want an ice cream container, you have to eat some of what it holds.

TRY THIS!
Use paint samples on strips to make an inexpensive border around your bulletin board.

Bulletin Boards

Ask a custodian to lower your bulletin board to child height so children can work activities on the bulletin board. To determine child height, ask a child to stand in front of a wall, stick out an arm, and touch the wall. That point should be just a little above the center of the bulletin board. Instead of using pushpins you could try Velcro, or try covering the board with acetate and using markers.

Backpacks

Use old backpacks. Ask parents to send in the ones their children no longer use. Fill each one with center activities and hang them on the wall, put them on a shelf, or line them up on the floor against a wall. Label them with the contents. When it is center time, the children choose a backpack and begin.

Large Gift Bags

At craft stores you can purchase large gift bags with handles to store center activities. Use sturdy bags and laminate them. Cut off or extend the handles before laminating the bags. If you cut off the handles, set them aside. You'll use them later.

Laminate the bags and trim them so they will open fully. To laminate a bag, run a closed bag through the laminator. Cut the laminating film to open the folded bottom, and cover that area with clear packing tape. If the bag has handles or straps, cut

SANITY SAVERS

them off before laminating, and re-attach them afterward. Laminating strengthens the bag and makes it more durable in the classroom. Fill the bag with center activities. Each bag becomes a center.

💡 Backs of Doors

Don't forget the bare backs of doors. They are great places for hanging flat items such as posters, interactive charts, and songs. Attach with Sticky Tac.

💡 Clothesline

Hang a clothesline under the chalkboard. Tie 12-inch lengths of red and green ribbon about every 20", alternating each color. The green ribbon means "start." The red ribbon means "stop" (see illustration). Tie a clothespin to the end of each green ribbon. Make a label for each center and hang each label from the clothespin on each of the green ribbons (for example, "Games and Puzzles," "Art," and "Math"). Put the activities in resealable plastic bags and hang them between the green and red ribbons. Children can stand in that spot and work at the chalkboard.

The green ribbon tells a child where an activity begins; the red tells him where it ends. The label tells the child where to return the bag when he is finished using it. Make sure to securely fasten the clothesline and ribbons because children play with these activities often.

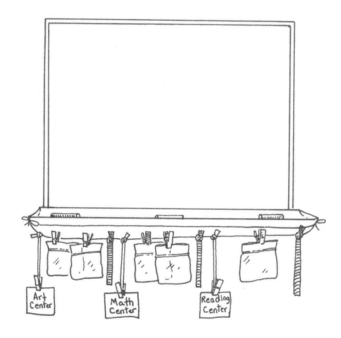

TRY THIS!
If a drawer sticks, wax the edge of the runners with wood wax or soap.

Chest of Drawers

An old chest of drawers makes a wonderful place for storing centers because drawers can separate the centers. Soap the drawer runners so the children can open and close them easily. Store each activity in a drawer in a resealable plastic bag. Label the drawer and attach a picture or photograph next to the label. Put a smaller version of the picture on the bag. The labeling lets the children know where to return the activity.

Envelopes

Purchase heavy-duty envelopes of different colors to use for storing center activities. Laminate and trim the envelopes before you use them for activity storage. Divide up the envelopes by color so that all the green ones, for example, are for the Library Center, the red ones are for the Games and Puzzles Center, and so on.

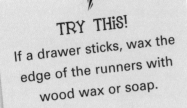

Put one activity in each envelope. Draw the activity on the outside of the envelope or take a photograph of the assembled activity and attach it. The colored envelope and the drawing or photograph give the children two clues about which activity goes in what envelope and where to return the envelopes when they are finished. Put the envelopes in baskets and put the baskets on a shelf.

Activities are easy to store in a filing cabinet. Store the envelopes by color and add a similarly-colored labeled divider. The color coding helps you identify the center and lets you know where to return the envelopes.

IDEAS FROM SHARON
You may not have thought about it, but box-to-lid matching is a useful learned skill. Skills like this are helpful tools for teaching reading, writing, and math skills.

Shoeboxes

Shoeboxes are useful and easy to find. Use ½" bolts with nuts, duct tape, or brads to join four or five boxes together. The grouping of boxes makes one center (the illustration on the next page is of a Science Center).

At center time, put a group of boxes on a table. Shoeboxes stack easily and the children can manage them well. Mark the box lids so the children can match the lids to the correct box.

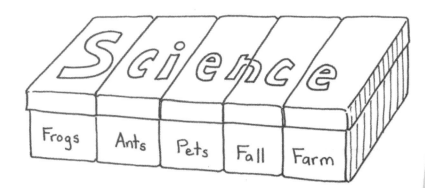

TRY THIS!
Half- and one-inch "through" bolts with matching nuts are a wonderful addition to the classroom. I like the #10 bolt and matching nut. You can bolt ice cream buckets, shoeboxes, and cardboard boxes together. Buy the bolts and nuts at hardware stores or home improvement stores.

Rolling Baskets

Rolling carts with baskets are an expensive addition to the small classroom, but they offer so much flexibility that it's hard to live without them. Some carts are made with a wooden, cutting board top that can be used to store another basket of center activities.

These carts allow centers to be easily maneuvered to new locations and rolled around the classroom floor. In the small-room scheme, each cart typically has three baskets; each basket is one center. The center operates like this: The child rolls a cart to a table and the Art Center basket is removed and the center is set up. The child then moves to the next location and sets up the next center, and so on. When it is time to clean up, roll the cart out and collect the baskets.

Sweater Boxes

Shallow, clear plastic sweater boxes aren't cheap, but they have multiple uses and they give you lots of storage choices in a small room setting. For one thing, they stack well in unusual places, like under a table. Store activities in resealable, clear plastic bags, label them, and layer them in the bottom of each box.

💡 Tabletop Easels

Tabletop easels are the only way to go in a small room. They collapse easily and they store flat. When they really get yucky, you can just toss them out. Fold cardboard as shown in the illustration, attach yarn to keep the easel standing, and hot glue two clothespins to the cardboard.

💡 Drying Racks

What to do with those dripping wet, gluey things? Make a drying rack from shallow boxes, just like the one in the illustration.

💡 Art Shelves

No shelves at all? Make your own. Use the picture directions in the illustration to make all you need. Use the leftover nuts and bolts you bought for the shoeboxes to make art shelves.

💡 Marker, Crayon, and Paper Holder

Look for a special sale of dish drying racks at a discount store. Buy two or three racks and two silverware holders for each rack. Use the silverware holders to store markers and crayons. Store file folders in the dish racks. The dish racks also offer you storage for all kinds of 9" x 12" paper for the Art Center and for children's books in the Library Center. The rack also works well in the Writing Center for pencil and paper. The racks store easily; just take out the silverware holders and stack the racks.

We are at the end of the small room chapter. You know you can make it in a small room—if you're organized and you have a plan. Now, add noise. Turn the page to find quiet.

Teacher Resources

Creating Child-Centered Classrooms edited by Pamela Coughlin
Hard Facts on Smart Classroom Designs by Daniel Niemeyer

Children are loud. Knowing this has made me more patient with children and the noise they make. There are times, however, when children need to be less noisy. When these occasions occur, young children's attention can be captured using certain tricks of the trade.

TRY THIS!

Work for the hum. A noisy, humming classroom tells you that the children are learning. Take the noise up a couple of notches, however, and some may feel that things are out of control. While that may not be the case, it is hard to convince another teacher who is upset by the noise.

The following quieting techniques will work marvelously to bring the noise level down in your classroom. If you use them too often, however, the children will expect them and they will no longer work. So use these suggestions sparingly to prolong their effectiveness!

PVC Pipe

Use a PVC-pipe "sound phone" to teach phonics (it helps children hear word sounds without noise interference from the classroom). I used it one day in an unusual way. It came to mind in desperation—the room was rocking with noise. I felt I had to do something to avoid immediate removal from my classroom.

At the time, I had the sound phone in my hand. I lifted it to my ear and said:

"Hello! Yes, this is Sharon MacDonald. Who is this? Oh, hi, how are you? Sure. Thanks for calling. Talk to you later. Bye."

I removed the phone from my ear and set it on the table.

"Who was it?" asked one of the children.

"Yeah, who was it?" said several others.

"Is this a real phone?" I asked.

"No," they said.

"But who was it?" asked one.

"It was our neighbor," I replied.

"What did they want?' asked another.

"They wanted to know if we could keep the noise down."

Some of the children nodded blankly and resumed work. Others looked at me and smiled.

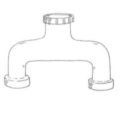

For the rest of the day the classroom was quieter. For a moment, I marveled at my quick thinking. Then, I smiled at how young children are so eager and willing to pretend that my sound phone was a telephone. I wondered if they really believed me. But, maybe they spent the rest of the day thinking about their silly teacher who answered telephone calls on her PVC-pipe phone.

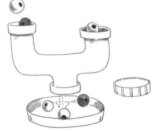

TRY THIS!

Use a PVC-pipe "plumbing elbow" with a drain hole and threaded cap at the elbow to teach combining sets. Use different colored beads to pour in either end of the elbow. The children unscrew the drain plug to extract the beads: Three green beads plus two red beads equals five beads. Children love learning math this way.

🔆 The Smile on a Stick

A "smile-on-a-stick" is fun to raise to your face. Draw different smiles; put each one on a jumbo craft stick. When the noise level is high, choose a smile from your collection and walk around the room with it placed just below your nose. It looks funny, and it captures the children's attention. They focus on you long enough for you say, "We are getting noisy. Can we lower the noise level please?"

🔆 Rain Stick

A rain stick makes the sound of rain falling gently when turned from end to end. Ask the noisiest child to be the rain stick girl or boy and walk around the classroom turning it on one end and then on the other. It is remarkable how two or three rounds through the classroom reduces the noise.

🔆 Soft Music

Many teachers use soft music to lower the noise level. Soft, classical music works well sometimes but only when the children can hear it. If they can't hear because it is too noisy, try something else first, and then try the classical music.

🔆 Pattern Clapping

Loudly clap out a pattern that the children know well. Gradually soften the clap until everyone is clapping with you and then transition to a silent clap. Ask for them to return to work when they are clapping silently. An added benefit of pattern clapping is that it helps the children develop patterning skills, which are essential in learning to read, do math, and develop skills across curriculum.

An example of a pattern clap that the children would know: clap, clap/clap, clap, clap/clap, clap, clap/clap, clap, and so on.

TRY THIS!
Make the following "smiles-on-a-stick": handlebar mustache, hot lips, and an open mouth. Keep them in your collection. And remember, anything on a stick can be a puppet.

IDEAS FROM SHARON
Children want to please the important adults in their lives. When they don't, it is mostly because they don't know how.

IDEAS FROM SHARON
Sometimes there is no particular reason why some ideas don't work in the classroom. Simply try something else and see what happens.

Simon Says

Stop for a minute to play Simon Says. It refocuses the children's attention, and afterward you can suggest they get back to work.

Puppets

Use a puppet to discuss the noise level in the room. One little puppet can convey to the whole class that it is too noisy. Use puppets rather than other toys because the children know that you are the one talking, but they watch in amazement, as the puppet comes to life in your hand.

A good puppeteer will let herself get lost in the moment and be "a really sleepy puppet," for example, that "can't go back to bed because of all the noise." Another approach might be for you to take a puppet over to a particularly noisy child. Hand a puppet to the child and ask him to discuss how he feels about all the noise in the room. Often, this brings down the noise to a conversation level and the noise subsides in the room.

Measuring Tape

Purchase a retractable tape measure and do some pretend measurements with the class. Pretend, for instance, to "measure" the noise in the room. Tell the children that the noise is six feet tall! Challenge them to lower the noise to "two feet." Measure horizontally and vertically.
Sometimes you will get two feet vertically, but not horizontally (two children in the corner are still carrying on, for example). As the noise subsides, retract the tape. This is one of the best noise interventions I have used.

Pretend Games

Make up pretending games, such as giving each child a piece of pretend bubble gum. Act out the movements of chewing and blowing bubbles. The children become so occupied with chewing that they stop talking. The noise level in the classroom comes down.

Give a noisy child a chance to "hold a quiet bug" and pass it on to someone who is quiet enough to hold it too.

Use your finger to dispense "quiet gasoline." "Fill up" a noisy child with quiet gas. Approach the child, point your finger to his ear and make a sound like he is being filled up with gasoline. If the noise continues, ask the child, "Do you need more quiet gas? Do you think you might have sprung a leak?"

"I Can Help" Book

Often, the source of noise is a frustrated child. Sometimes a child cannot get a job done quickly enough for his own satisfaction. The "I Can Help" book is a place a child can go to get help from another child when you are involved with something or someone else. The book reduces frustration and anxiety in the child—and the noise—and makes for a much smoother day all around. Using the "I Can Help" book teaches children to depend on themselves and other children, not always on you.

Use each book page to describe what other children in the class can do. For example, who can tie a shoe? Take a photograph of a child tying her shoe, label it "I can tie," and put in the book. When a child can tie, she puts her name in the book. The addition of a name to a page in the book means that she also is willing to tie the shoes of others. Other children can add their names as they learn to tie and can help others. Other pages might be:

- I can turn and hold the water fountain handle.
- I can open the high-cabinet door.
- I can button.
- I can snap.
- I can braid.
- I can zip.
- I can help with the days of the week.
- I can help with the months of the year.
- I can help count to ___.
- I can pour.

💡 Hand Signals

My class developed a few unique hand signals that reminded the class to lower the noise. Anyone in the class could initiate the signal if they thought it was too loud in the room. Other children then used the signal and lowered their voices. We changed signals often.

💡 Quiet Words

Ask the children to think of quiet words. Tell them you are making a list of quiet words and walk around the room to collect them. The noisier children can be asked directly to contribute quiet words. Asking the children to spend more time thinking than talking will reduce the noise level.

💡 "Sing/Quiet" Sign

Make a double-sided sign with "Sing" on the front and "Quiet" on the back. Teach the children that "Quiet" means that they sing inside their heads. Begin by showing them how to use the sign. Start a song, hold up the sign, and turn it from "Sing" to "Quiet" during the song. Do it often. Using the sign gets the children thinking about what quiet sounds like. It also gives you quiet time between the noise to mention lowering the noise level. You can ask them to be quiet without raising your voice over their noise.

Once the children learn to sing out loud when the "Sing" sign is displayed and to sing in their heads when the "Quiet" sign is displayed, you are ready to use it to reduce the noise level in the classroom. Display the "Quiet" sign for longer and longer periods of time. My class would sing about two words a line and sing in their heads for the rest of the time. This noisy room intervention works best when you are getting ready to clean up or to leave the classroom.

💡 Noisemaker

Find a noisemaker that makes silly sounds, such as a bicycle horn, a wind-up music box, or a Halloween or New Year's noisemaker. When the class gets rowdy, use the noisemaker to get their attention. Ask for quiet. The noisemaker gets their attention without you having to say much. On the occasions that you ask for quiet, remember to smile. The children will respond in the same way.

IDEAS FROM SHARON
Songs keep us sane,
so sing!

Silent

Sing!

The noisemaker approach has backfired from time to time. Sometimes it gets them more excited, especially if they are excited already, like before a field trip. During the ride, the children may make noisemaker sounds all the way to the site and back again. It can make for a long day!

Remote Control

Find an old TV remote control. When the noise gets high, walk around the room and tell the children you would like to lower the sound with the remote. As you press the buttons, tell the children you are lowering the volume, and they will make their voices softer. After they get the hang of it, let another child operate the remote volume control.

Songs

Songs are the best noise-reduction tools. Start singing. The whole class will join you.

It's quiet now. But when you turn the page, the noise and confusion will start over again-we will be going through "Transitions."

Teacher Resources

Practical Solutions to Practically Every Problem by Steffen Saifer
There's Got to Be a Better Way by Becky Bailey

Transitions are times during the day when children change either location or activity. Transitions can be familiar and easy or unfamiliar and difficult.

Transitions from home to school, from one place in the school to another, and from school to home are the biggest challenges of all. Successful transitions are at the heart of managing a successful classroom.

We can look to philosophy to offer guidance on how to handle transitions. Chinese history is rich with philosophical gems of personal experience with transitions and teaching the young.

Remember the old public speaking adage: "Tell them what you're going to say, say it, then tell them what you said" (Chinese in origin, author unknown). It's exhausting, but it is the essence of teaching and of moving from one place to the next.

TRANSITIONS TO SCHOOL

Starting school is a scary thing for a young child. For many children, it is the first significant transition from home since they were born. Even those who have previous experience have anxiety about school. Children pick up on school's importance, and enter with much apprehension, so starting the school year positively is what is important for most children. Try a few of the following ideas to ease tension at transition time.

TRY THIS!

The most "loyal and trustworthy" copiers have names. Ask your class to select some names and vote on one. It is important that the children value a copy of their original work, because you will want to collect many of their originals for assessment purposes (to put in their portfolios). Young children may not want to give you their work—they want to take it home! If you do a good job of singing the praises of copies, however, you should get the originals without objection.

School Visits

Encourage parents to bring their child to school to visit the classroom before the school year starts.

Home Visits

If school policy permits, make a home visit with a small toy or a game from one of the centers. Help the child return the toy to where it belongs in the classroom on his first day at school.

Postcards

Send postcards home inviting the children to your classroom.

Tour the Building

Tour the school with the children on the first day. Introduce the children to school staff, to other classes nearby, and show them things in the school such as the copier machine.

Bubbles

Purchase a bubble-blowing bottle necklace for each child. When the children arrive, give out the necklaces and ask them to put them on. When they feel sad or homesick, suggest that they blow bubbles—it really does make them feel better.

☀ "Friends-and-Family" Board

Encourage parents to send a picture of the family (not all family members need to be in the picture). Label the board "Friends and Family" and put up the pictures. The children can visit the board when they get homesick.

☀ Telephone

Take a few minutes before school starts to telephone each child and introduce yourself. Talk about one fun aspect of school.

☀ Photograph

Mail a picture of one of the centers in your room to each child; when the child arrives, ask him to find the center.

☀ Happy Rock

Give each child a penny-size piece of paper. Take the children outside to find a rock the same size as the paper. Give the children a couple of days to get to know the rock. Ask each child to give his rock a name. Suggest that he examine his rock with a magnifying glass, weigh it, draw it, write about it, discuss it with his peers, wash it with a toothbrush, measure it, and tell his family the history of his rock. After the children get to know their rocks well, have them put the rocks in a shoebox lid for a visit to their teacher's house over the weekend.

> **TRY THIS!**
> Read Byrd Baylor's book, *Everybody Needs a Rock*, to the children. It gives the children an introduction to rocks and how to hunt for a special rock outside.

Take the rocks home and draw a happy face on each rock with a black permanent marker. Bring all the rocks back to school on Monday. Ask each child to find his rock among all the other rocks. Amazingly, each child will find his very own—some will talk to it as if it were a pet.

Read to the children the following "Happy Rock Story" so they will understand why there is a smile on their rocks.

Happy Rock Story
By Sharon MacDonald

Here is your happy rock!
Rub it and the smile on it gradually fades.
But the smile walks right up your arm and to your face.
It jumps on your mouth and slips onto your lips.
The smile picks up your lips, and your teeth show.
Now you know how to smile!

Keep the rocks in the shoebox lid. Explain that the rocks are happier and more comfortable together. Whenever a child is feeling a little sad he can go get his happy rock and rub. Soon a smile will walk right up his arm and slip onto his lips.

IDeas FROM SHaRON

On difficult days, teachers benefit from blowing bubbles. If you like to do a lot of bubble blowing, like I do, wait until the children are gone for the day.

TRANSITIONS DOWN THE HALL

Moving from the classroom to the hallways and then down the hall is the hardest transition of all. You need "travelin'" music but you can't play it because the other classes will hear it. The hall seems to say to the children, "Run, run!" You say, "Walk, walk...Quiet! Whisper." It doesn't do much good. Because nothing structured is happening, the children structure the time for themselves by talking, laughing, pushing, and playing. It's a natural thing for children to do. You need a few techniques and tricks for getting children down the hall without disturbing other classes. Try some of these ideas.

Songs

Use songs that lend themselves to transitions. These are quiet, calm songs. Encourage children to sing with their "inside-of-your-head voice" or to sing at a whisper. To find some good songs to use, try looking for children's CDs with relevant music, such as *Quiet Times* by Greg and Steve or *Sleepy Time* by Dr. Thomas Moore.

As with marching, the key to successful transitions with young children is time. Give children time to prepare to move. Before exiting the room, you must prepare them to exit the room.

"Quiet Lotion"

As you are headed out the door, give children a little hand lotion. Ask them to rub it in as they walk. It gives them something structured to do so that they will pass down the hall more quietly. This works well.
Caution: Be sure that none of the children in your class are allergic to hand lotion. Ask a family member to test it at home.

TRY THIS!
Quiet Lotion can become Problem-Solving Lotion—just change the label on the bottle! When a child is having a hard time solving a problem, put a little hand lotion in the palm of his hand. Ask him to rub it in well, think about the problem, and see if he can come up with a solution all by himself. Keep a large pump-dispenser bottle of hand lotion available to refill the small jars.

💡 Heavy Load

Sam is the child in the middle of the classroom blowing the referee's whistle. The rest of the children have their fingers in their ears. I am not being heard. What to do? Prepare for Sam.

Each of us has had children in our classrooms who challenge us more than others. In my case, it was Sam. I said Sam's name 100 times a day. When I came up with a plan for anything, I always asked myself, "Is this Sam-proof?" or "How am I going to manage Sam?" I wanted Sam to be successful in school, but to get that done I had to reduce the opportunities Sam had for inventive, but disruptive, behavior.

One of the biggest challenges was getting down the hall with Sam. What often worked well was giving Sam something awkward enough to carry that it required both hands and most of his attention to get it down the hall without knocking down a wall display or hitting a coat rack. I settled on a tub of outdoor toys (most of the time). Since Sam's hands were occupied and his attention was focused, he aimed himself down the hallway and, more often than not, completed his transition uneventfully. He also felt special because he had helped.

💡 Pretend Games

This is a helpful way to move down the hall with children. Try these:

■ Let's pretend we are mice and tiptoe silently.
■ Let's fly quietly, like an owl or a butterfly, down the hall and out the door.
■ Let's pretend we are detectives trying to find footprints on the floor with our pretend magnifying glasses.
■ Flow down the hall like a river.
■ Let's fly on our quiet magic carpet.
■ Make our fingers soft—make them fall like rain as we walk.
■ Walk like the "Elastic Man."
■ Float like a balloon.
■ Crawl like a snail.
■ Walk softly like a cat.
■ Walk through the mud, or on thin ice, or on hot coals.

Be creative! Be interesting. Have fun. Let the children make suggestions. They are great at pretending!

Circus-Parade Spacing

Walking down the hall requires proper spacing between the children so that they don't step on each other's heels. Young children, however, do not quite grasp the concept of or the need for an orderly line. It is worth the time it takes to explain that people need space between them to keep from stepping on each other when they walk. "It is like at the circus," I say. "At the circus they use "circus spacing." The distance between the animals is how the ringmaster keeps the animals in a parade. What would happen if all the animals ran into each other during the parade?" I ask. "We need to space ourselves, one arm length from the person in front." It works (some of the time)!

As an alternative, ask the children to line up on carpet squares. Put a letter of the alphabet on each carpet square and assign each child a letter for the week. Line up the squares end-to-end. The child finds his assigned letter and stands on that square. This starts them off down the hall at a good distance from one another.

Hand Signs

Help the children make up their own sign language so that they can talk with their hands. It is fun to see what signs they come up with. Ask them to practice their sign language a lot. Make a big chart of signs and put them up in the classroom. Hand signs effectively lower the noise level during difficult transitions, like going down the hall. Ask the children to talk using only their signs when they are in the hall.

You could also teach the children the American Sign Language alphabet. Put up a poster of the alphabet and encourage the children to try to sign words. Teach them the signs for a few words such as "hello" and "quiet."

Map

Make a map of the school during the first week and show it to the children. Use a timer to see how long it takes to get from place to place. Put the times on the school map. Talk to the children about how easy it is to walk quietly for two minutes when we know it is only a two-minute walk. Set a timer in the classroom and practice being quiet for two minutes. The children will see that they can do it. The first few times you walk, take the timer with you so the children can see the time ticking away. They will know they can talk soon, so it will be easier for them to keep quiet.

Follow the Leader

Play this game as you move down the hall. Just be sure to choose a calm leader who will model quiet behavior, like pretend games (see page 94).

Hips and Lips

One of my workshop participants shared the following idea. It is called "hips and lips." The children put four fingers of one hand on their lips and their other hand on their hips. They "swish" down the hall like dancers.

IDEAS FROM SHARON
A helpful book for handling transitions is *Transition Time* by Jean Feldman.

END-OF-THE-DAY TRANSITIONS

Because you don't know where you are sending them at the end of the day, and what will be asked of them when they get there, you need to send them out feeling successful, positive, and at ease. You can do it if you have a plan. Here are some ideas for a happy ending to your day.

Whole-Group Closure

Closing the day calmly helps everyone feel good about the day. Closing the day hurriedly revs up children and can cause unnecessary tension. For instance, don't get caught five minutes before dismissal with a messy room. You will rush around trying to get things in order. The children will copy what you do. Chaos will ensue. If you're like me, you will start to issue orders to the children. The day ends abruptly without anyone feeling good about what they have done that day.

SANITY SAVERS

💡 Alarm Clock

Set an alarm clock for 15-20 minutes before school ends. You'll have time for closure and a smooth, unhurried exit. Gather the children together, talk about the day's events, and let the children discuss different aspects of the day. They will slowly calm down and get ready to leave. Here are some closing questions you might use:

- What did you learn today?
- Where did you work today (in what center)?
- What was your favorite part of the day?
- What was your least favorite part of the day?
- What are you going to share with your parents today?
- What new things did you do today?
- Who did you work with today?
- Who helped you today?
- What do you think tomorrow will be like?

💡 Line-Up Pictures

Designate places for the children to line up in groups for their buses. They will learn where to stand. Give the numbered buses names that the children are familiar with. For example, call "Bus 32" the "Dog" bus. Put a drawing or a picture of a dog on the wall above where the children line up. Use other animals for each of the other buses. Include the bus number so that if a child has trouble finding his bus, he can tell another teacher which bus he rides. If parents pick up some children, designate a place where those children will wait.

| Bus 32 | Bus 9 | Bus 24 | Bus 17 |
| Dog Group | Mouse Group | Duck Group | Cat Group |

Singing

If the children are taking home materials, send them in groups of four to collect supplies, and sing songs with the rest of the children. Develop this routine and the children will go for the materials spontaneously when you point to the next four children. You will not have to stop singing because the children know what to do.

Notes

Put notes for families in envelopes; pin the envelopes to the children's shirts. To remind you to send notes and materials home, tack a large envelope to the wall near the door. Put all of your notes and school-to-home materials in it. Hand them out as the children go out the door for the day.

Backpack Yarn

If your class uses backpacks, put the notes inside and ask the children to tie an 18- to 24-inch length of yarn to the backpacks. The yarn is a reminder that a note is inside. For children who cannot yet tie, ask other children to help them. Encourage the children to return the yarn to school. The returned yarn helps you to know that someone at home read your note.

You may think you're done with the week, but you aren't. Turn the page for "Cooking Fridays."

Teacher Resources

Teachable Transitions by Rae Pica

Terrific Transitions by Ellen Booth Church

Transition Magician by Nola Larson, Mary Henthorne, and Barbara Plum

Transition Magician 2 by Mary Henthorne, Nola Larson, and Ruth Chvojicek

Transition Tips and Tricks by Jean Feldman

Transition Time by Jean Feldman

I always cooked on Friday afternoons because I was ready for the weekend, and I needed a little "pepping up" to get through the last hour or so of the day.

Teaching is hard work, especially on Fridays. Cooking renewed my interest and piqued my attention when both were flagging in the middle of the afternoon. Cooking is also a wonderful way to teach children to learn to read and write and to do science and math. The nose and the mouth are the shortest "distance" to the brain.

Chapter 9

COOKING FRIDAYS

IDEAS FROM SHARON

Pay attention to how you feel. There is a good chance that the children feel just like you do. If you're bored, so are they. So, do something different.

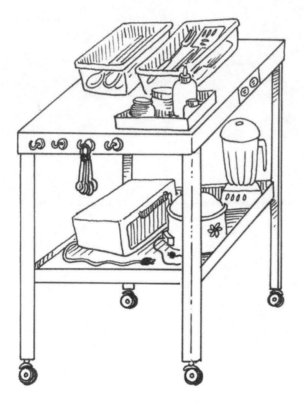

Most children like food. Cooking in the classroom is almost always received enthusiastically. As I mentioned earlier, it is a wonderful way to teach many different skills. The downside? Cooking is messy and it is hard for each child to have a turn. The benefits outweigh the obstacles, however. You can run a comb through a knotted Friday afternoon by taking the top off the electric skillet and cooking something! This chapter, though it does not include recipes, may help your cooking time with the children become more valuable and educational. Here's how to start:

Draw and enlarge the recipe picture directions you use in the classroom so the children can see them from a distance. That way, you can work on reading, math, science, and social studies while cooking in a large group. Also, enlarge the recipes so the children can "read" them. They will associate what you say with the print. Experiment with recipes and try to remember what works best when you use cooking as a teaching tool.

Step 1 — Wash the strawberry

Step 2 — Pull off the top.

Step 3 — Share with a friend.

Step 4 — Eat!

Cooking is always messy and there will be Friday afternoons that will make you wonder why you selected this particular Friday to cook. You can, however, simplify things to the point that the undertaking is more than "livable." For example, you can wash a carrot, peel it, and eat it. Bon appetit!

💡 Moveable Cooking Cart

Find an old A-V cart no one is using and make it into a cooking cart. Put larger appliances on the bottom two shelves: an electrical skillet, a crock-pot, a small toaster oven, a blender, a cutting board, and a small burner and saucepan, and stackable, large mixing bowls.

TRY THIS!
If you use metal measuring spoons and cups, put red fingernail polish on the handles of each of the measuring spoons, over the fractions (1 tablespoon, 1 teaspoon, ½ teaspoon, ¼ teaspoon). This makes the measuring units easier to read. You can also do this to your plastic measuring tools.

IDEAS FROM SHARON
While what you really need is a dream kitchen in your classroom, you may have been told that it can't happen this year. How about a rolling, double-level cooking cart?

Put the smaller cooking utensils in clear plastic boxes (about the size of shoeboxes) and store them on the top shelf. Keep the condiments, food coloring, and spices in a box by themselves. Put flatware, jumbo craft sticks (for stirring), measuring spoons, small measuring cups, manual can openers, and several potato peelers in another box. Keep sharp knives in a location other than the cooking cart, so that only you can reach them when needed. *(continued on the next page)*

Put wax paper, clear plastic wrap, toothpicks, plastic utensils, paper napkins, and dessert-size paper plates in another box. Attach magnetic hooks around the metal sides on the top shelf. On the hooks, hang large utensils: a whisk, a large stirring spoon, spatulas, an oven mitt, a vegetable brush, and a cookie sheet.

 Dishtowel Apron

It is hard to find tie-at-the-waist aprons. Make your own with a dishtowel and a 36-inch length of heavy-duty string. It doesn't cost as much either.

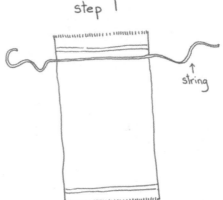

step 1

string

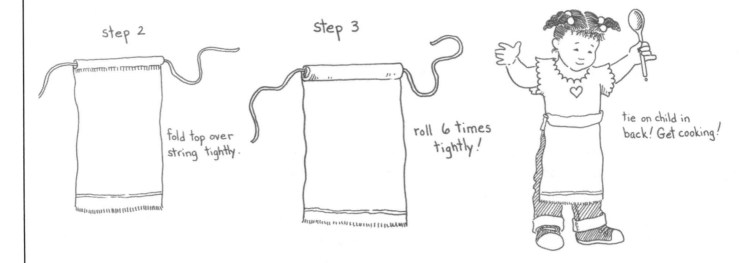

step 2

fold top over string tightly.

step 3

roll 6 times tightly!

tie on child in back! Get cooking!

Tables of Measurement and Equivalents

This table helps with the math of cooking measurement. Having these equivalents is helpful, too, if you don't have all of your measuring cups on hand. Lots of measuring cups mysteriously end up in strange places in the classroom.

IDEAS FROM SHARON
Pay attention to how you feel. There is a good chance that the children feel just like you do. If you're bored, so are they. So, do something different.

- A few grains is a little less than ⅛ of a teaspoon
- 60 drops is about 1 teaspoon and 15 drops are ¼ teaspoon
- 3 teaspoons are equal to 1 tablespoon
- 1 teaspoon is ⅓ tablespoon
- 2 tablespoons are equal to 1 fluid ounce
- 1 tablespoon is ½ fluid ounce
- 4 tablespoons are equal to ¼ cup
- 5⅓ tablespoons are equal to ⅓ cup
- 16 tablespoons are equal to 1 cup, which is 8 fluid ounces
- 1 pint of liquid is equal to 2 cups, or 16 fluid ounces
- 1 quart of liquid is equal to 2 pints, or 32 fluid ounces
- ½ gallon is equal to 2 quarts, or 64 ounces
- 1 gallon of liquid is equal to 8 pints, or 128 fluid ounces, or 4 quarts

When children cook, they learn math by measuring the ingredients, exploring the volume of the mixture, and counting the cups of ingredients and teaspoons of measurement. They count the raisins added, examine the numbers on the cans, and count out the number cookies each child in the class can have when they pass them out.

If they cut things into pieces they are dealing with part-whole relationships and beginning an exploration of division and fractions. The science happens with the math. One principle they learn, for example, is irreversible change; ingredients mixed together can never be taken apart again. They also have a chance to examine how much change took place and how long it took. That is measurement, and measurement is math. While cooking, children also learn to follow sequential steps, an essential science principle that is fundamental to scientific exploration.

The simple machines and utensils, like an electric skillet and spatula, help children learn about the value and importance of tools in making work easier. Science and math are rolled up into one fun and inviting process that captures the children's interest and enthusiasm for learning.

Can Sizes and Equivalent Amounts

This information is useful if your recipe calls for "a cup and a half" of something that is a solid in a can. Converting cups to cans can be confusing. I never knew how much was in the can so I never knew which size to buy. Some cans measure weight, others don't. Following is a table showing cans and equivalent amounts.

- 16 ounces is a pound.
- An 8-ounce can has 8 ounces of food inside and is equal to one cup.
- A 12-ounce vacuum-packed can actually does weigh 12 ounces, but it is only 1 ¼ cups rather than 1 ½ cups.
- A "Number 2" can weighs 20 ounces (1 pound, 4 ounces) and it is 2 ½ cups.
- A 15-ounce can of condensed milk is 2 ⅓ cups.
- Evaporated milk comes in 2 different-size cans; 6 and 14 ½ ounces. The 6-ounce can is ⅔ cup; the 14 ½ ounce is 1 ⅔ cups.

Substitute Ingredients

If you are like me, you always have all the ingredients you need—except one. You can't leave the classroom to buy what you need, so you have to use a substitute. Over the years I have combed through cookbooks and household hint books to find substitutes for various products. I kept the following list on one of my magnetic cart hooks, and I referred to it whenever I was missing an ingredient.

- ⅓ teaspoon baking soda with ½ teaspoon cream of tartar works like 1 teaspoon baking powder.
- 1 cup yogurt works like 1 cup buttermilk and vice versa.
- 3 tablespoons cocoa with 1 tablespoon butter equal 1 square of chocolate (and they usually end up in the recipe, whereas the chocolate square often does not).
- 4 tablespoons of powdered milk in 1 cup water does the same job as 1 cup milk or ½ cup evaporated milk.
- ½ cup water works almost as well as 1 cup milk.
- To make a cup of sour milk (to replace buttermilk), add 1 teaspoon vinegar or lemon juice to a cup of warm milk; let it sit for five minutes and pour.
- 1 cup applesauce can substitute for 1 cup butter.

Rice Krispie Treats and Sticky Hands

Rice Krispie Treats are a favorite of children. The recipe is right on the back of the box. The major problem was always that the children's hands would get so sticky that they couldn't get the mix out of the bowl into the pan. They would stand around trying to shake off the Rice Krispie lumps stuck to their hands. I learned to let them run their hands under cold water before they attempted to move the mix from the bowl to the pan. The extra moisture didn't hurt the recipe a bit.

Keeping Ants Away

Ants are a problem from time to time. At times it seemed as if they watched us cook and then pounced on the drippings. I found an interesting idea in Hints from Heloise: Surround what you want to "ant proof" with a chalk line. Heloise says ants won't cross a chalk line. Give it a try!

Safety

Some activities require appliances that you don't want the children to use alone or to touch. Make those activity areas safe by marking them. Begin by making copies of the children's hands and use the handprints to mark the appliances. Here is a good way to do that. During the first few days of school, introduce the children to the copy machine and make a photocopy of each child's pair of hands. Write each child's name along the bottom of the prints and recopy the entire stack. Give one copy to each child to take home; use the second copy for marking cooking activities.

When setting up a cooking activity, move an appliance (like an electric skillet or crock pot) from the cooking cart to a work area. Use colored masking tape to restrict an area around the appliance. Use one of the children's handprints to label the area.

Cut out a child's handprints, Jessica's for example, with the name clearly visible. Tape the prints to the table surface with red masking tape, making a circle with a line through it, inside the area defining the workspace. The handprints say to the children: this might burn you if you touch it. *(continued on the next page)*

The other children pay attention and so does Jessica. With her newfound status in the classroom community, she strolls around the room checking things out, reminding everyone not to touch the appliance with the red masking tape all around it. During the year, each child can have a turn at having his or her handprints used for this purpose.

Well, we "cooked" Fridays and nothing was burned. There are some "Leftover" things in the chapter ahead. See you on the next page.

Teacher Resources

Cooking Art by MaryAnn F. Kohl and Jean Potter
Kitchen Idea Bags by Sharon MacDonald
One Cup Cooking by Barbara Johnson and Betty Plemons
Snacktivities! by MaryAnn F. Kohl and Jean Potter

Sometimes the best part of a book is last. This book is not like that. Here, only good things become leftovers. Good stuff is in all of the chapters! In this chapter you will find delicious "leftovers"—the activities and ideas that did not fit very well into the other chapters. I am sure you will enjoy them along with the rest.

💡 Glue Bottles With Tops "Permanently" Sealed

All teachers know that old, half-full glue bottles seem to be sealed permanently. It is frustrating to throw away good glue simply because the bottle won't open. Pliers come to mind, I am sure, but in my early years I tore the tops off lots of bottles. Here is a different approach.

Set up a safe place away from the children. Fill a dishpan full of hot water and drop in all of your sealed glue bottles. Let them soak for one hour. Pour off some of the water, add more hot water, then turn the bottles over and soak them for another hour. Twist off the bottle tops by hand. If hand twisting doesn't work, gently twist with pliers. Peel off the dried glue and soak the tops in vegetable oil. If this approach does not work, throw away the glue bottles.

💡 "Yucky" Crayons

If your crayons look like they are all the same color, take heart. You can bring them back to life. Put a pie tin over a "warm" or "low" burner. Peel the paper off the crayons; use tongs to hold them over the pie tin (the tin catches the dripping wax). Turn the crayon so the "yucky" parts get most of the heat. The drippings create a crayon "pie" in the bottom of the tin. Let it stand. Break up the pie pieces and have the children use them to color.

Caution: Supervise this and any other activity involving heat. Always remember that safety comes first.

💡 Check-It-Out Table

Set up a small table for objects of interest—especially the ones the children bring to school to share with the other children in class. You can put things on the table to share, too.

Put a "Check It Out" sign with a large check mark sign above. Explain to the children that they can examine objects on the table that other children have brought to school. Each object will be on the table for three school days only. "Check It Out" is meant in two ways: (1) Carefully examine the object, and (2) take it home three days later.

Place the table against the wall. Collect trays of various-sizes, 3" x 5" index cards, pencils, and a large calendar with squares for each day of the month. Put the calendar on the wall at a child's eye level above the table. Stack the trays on the floor next to the table. Have the children choose the size of tray that best displays the object they have brought to school. Put the index cards in a small basket with the pencils.

Help the children label their objects with the index cards and put the cards on the tray next to the object. Use the calendar to mark each child's "check-in date" and a "check-out date" three days later. Help children remember to take their items home.

Gather tools for the children to examine the objects, like a stethoscope, ruler, tape measure, scale, magnifying glass, minifying glass, string, glasses, colored goggles, and other tools. Place these in a basket on the table.

For the older children, put out an Observation Form. The children can write or draw their observations on the form. You can use icons to designate different kinds of observations (see the illustrations on this page).

Book of Letters

Make a Book of Letters to use for the children's writings. It gives you a place to put all the wonderful notes, messages, and drawings you receive each morning.

Use a three-inch, three-ring binder with acetate sleeves and cardstock. Put one page of cardstock in each sleeve and put the sleeves in the binder. Tell the children this story:

Long ago there were just a few people who could read and write. Those who wrote created the art form of writing called calligraphy. The people who wrote were called calligraphers. Calligraphers would spend days writing a letter because they wanted the individual alphabetical letters to be formed perfectly and for the letter, as a whole, to be beautiful to look at.

Letters have an interesting past. Over 100 years ago, it took three months for a letter to travel by Pony Express from California to Boston, and it cost $20. People were thrilled when they got a letter. They so treasured them that they stored them in cedar boxes and layered each page of the letter with onionskin. Letters were read over and over again. When guests came to visit for an evening, they would pass the time by reading all the letters sent from others near and far away.

Today we don't store letters in cedar boxes and we don't use onionskin for letters. We send cards, talk on the phone, and even use computers to talk to one another. But there is a way to store our notes and drawings so they can be shared with others—binders with acetate sleeves. When you have a note and drawing that you want to share with everyone in the class, put them in the "Book of Letters." Your friends can read them and share the information, just like long ago.

The Book of Letters also has a second purpose. It shows that you value what they have written and brought to school. At the same time, it answers the question about where to keep the children's writings. They are all in one place to read and re-read over time. It also is a convenient storage place for the children's writings. You can refer to it for assessment purposes.

Hall-of-Fame Frame

Make Hall-of-Fame Frames to display the work of one or more children each week. Use old overhead frames (or make them from heavy construction paper). You'll need leftover laminating film, plastic tape, and overhead transparencies, too.

Make a Hall-of-Fame Frame for each child. Attach a transparency to the front of the overhead frame. Cover the back of the frame with laminating film attached to the frame's outer edge; trim the excess flush with the frame edge. Use clear plastic tape to attach the film to the back of the frame on three sides. Do not tape the top. The transparency will be on the front and the laminating film pocket will be on the back.

Once the frame is made, have each child decorate it with stickers and write his name on it. Put small pieces of hook-side Velcro on the back. In the hallway, at children's eye level, put a long strip of soft-side Velcro. To display them, press the frames against the Velcro strip.

Have a box in the classroom with a folder for each child. Write on each folder, "Hall of Fame." During the week, the children put the papers they are most proud of in their folders. On Fridays (or at a time that best suits your schedule) have the children select one paper from their folders that shows something they learned or accomplished. Display their papers in the Hall-of-Fame Frames in the hallway, leaving them up all week. Change the papers in the frames once a week. Keep all the Hall-of-Fame Frame papers taken from the frame during the year. At the end of the year, get a three-prong folder for each child, hole-punch the pages, and put all of the selected work in the folder to take home. The children are always so surprised and delighted with how far they have come during the year.

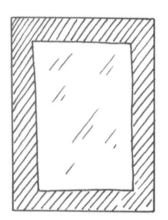

front

back

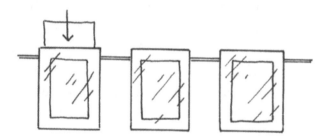

"Talking" Wall

A "talking" wall is a wall of events. It is a history of what happened in class. Each week, cut a six-foot strip of butcher paper and tape it beneath the chalkboard. Put a basket of pens, pencils, crayons, and markers nearby. Each day during center time, ask the children to document what has been going on in their classroom by writing and drawing on the butcher paper. They can record events such as a lost tooth, spilled paint, a field trip, a fire truck at school, a new classroom game, or a child's birthday. Make sure they document what is happening at school only, not what is going on at home or in the neighborhood, for instance. Trim the edges on Friday and put it up in the hall on a bulletin board. Change it each week. Over the course of the year, the classroom history becomes a decorative and informative landmark for other children and teachers in the school, who will enjoy knowing what is going on in your classroom. Other classrooms may even start a talking wall of their own.

The Answerer

Often, you'll have a child in your classroom who answers every question. These children are fast thinkers and, in the developmental sense, are ahead of many of the other children in the class. However, because the other children are not given enough time to think, they miss out on opportunities to participate in class discussions. To keep the answering child from speaking too quickly, take him aside before the day begins. Explain that you are going to ask questions that he can probably answer. Ask him to let other children say the answer (because everyone likes to have a turn) while he gives the answer with a secret signal to let you know that he knows the answer. Usually, I ask him to hold up his fingers in a "V" or to pat himself on the back so that I can see.

Sanity Saver Bottle

Use the Sanity Saver Bottle to help children calm down a little or to re-focus on what they need to be doing. Make a sanity saver bottle by filling an 8-ounce, plastic bottle two-thirds full with sand, seashells, beads, sequins, small pebbles, small stars, and a penny.

Ask a child who needs to calm down to find the penny in the bottle. Prepare a special place for them to find the penny, such as a small beanbag chair, a "Quiet House" (see below), or a rocker. The child rolls the bottle around until he finds the penny. It usually takes a little while. This time with the penny in a bottle gives the child time to calm down and unwind. Frustrations and disappointments are forgotten in pursuit of the penny.

securely sealed!

Name Labels

During the first four weeks of school, it is important that the children learn how to get along in the classroom together and what your expectations are (see Chapter 1, pages 15-20). Teaching children to write their names is not a high priority. What is important during this period is getting names on all of the work that the children produce. Use a short cut: Buy a box of computer address labels, type a page for each child, and put it in his folder. Whenever a child does work that he needs to put his name on, ask him to go to his folder, pull off a label, and stick it on his work.

Quiet House

Make a quiet place in your classroom for children who need to get away from the class experience for a minute or two. Buy a small, plastic wading pool at a garage sale. Fill it with pillows. Buy a golf umbrella at a flea market, or have a parent donate an old one that is still safe. Turn the umbrella upside down and hang it from the ceiling, above the pool and out of the children's reach, with monofilament fishing line. Buy two shower curtain liners and hang them on each umbrella rib, through the hanger holes along the top of the curtain liner. The curtain will hang outside the pool, giving the child inside the feeling of privacy, while allowing you to see inside. Add books.

SANiTY SAVeRS

💡 Thermometer

Teaching children how a thermometer works is a challenge. Teaching them to count by fives and tens is not an easy task, either. What to do? Make a thermometer out of a snack-size, zipper-closure resealable plastic bag. Copy and cut out the paper thermometer below. Put it inside the plastic bag with the edge of the thermometer against the bag opening. Cut off the remaining bag. Use clear plastic tape to tape the bag closed. Draw an arrow on the zipper pull that points to the numbers on the paper thermometer. The children move the zipper up and down to match the temperature showing on an outside thermometer.

Special note: Thanks to a teacher at one of my workshops for anonymously sharing this idea with me.

Step 1

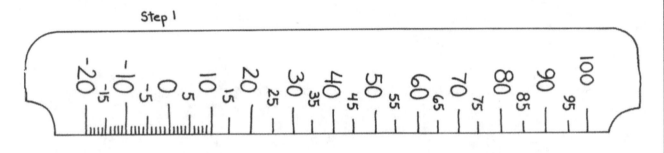

Step 2

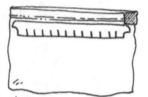

put inside zipper baggie
nearest the zipper.

Step 3

cut off excess.

step 4

Seal the open edge
with tape...fold over.

step 5

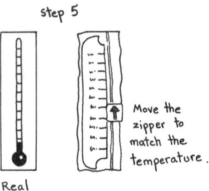

Real
thermometer

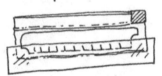

Move the
zipper to
match the
temperature.

Focus Goggles

Focus Goggles are "glasses" made from discarded, recycled pantyhose or "seconds" purchased from a manufacturer. See the illustration below for how to make them.

Use Focus Goggles to refocus a child's attention. It is a gentle, self-esteem-preserving way to give him a little help when he is having a "bumpy" day or to help the child hurdle an obstacle he is having difficulty getting over. The Focus Goggles may help him be less distracted or less frustrated, and he may feel more able to concentrate on completing a project.

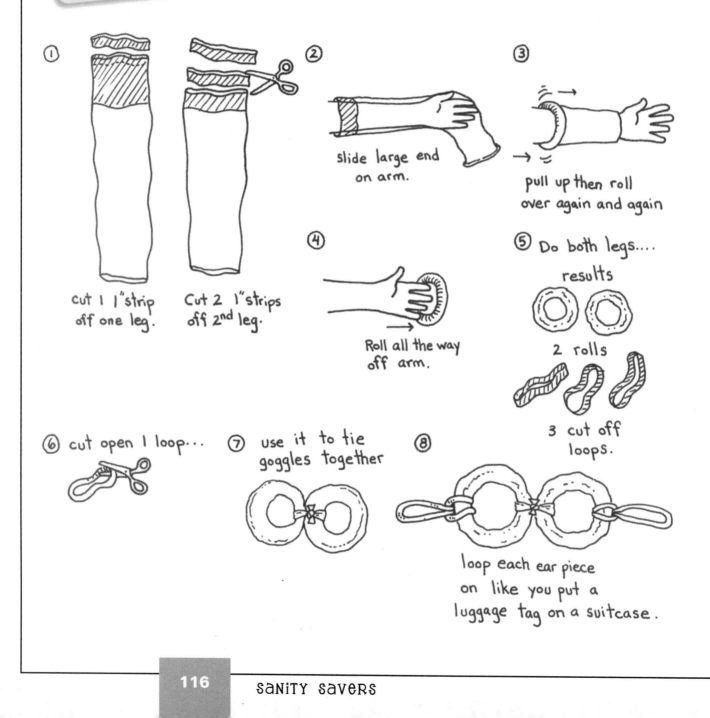

① cut 1 1" strip off one leg.   Cut 2 1" strips off 2nd leg.

② slide large end on arm.

③ pull up then roll over again and again

④ Roll all the way off arm.

⑤ Do both legs.... results   2 rolls   3 cut off loops.

⑥ cut open 1 loop...

⑦ use it to tie goggles together

⑧ loop each ear piece on like you put a luggage tag on a suitcase.

In the back of the book you will find that the inside of the back cover is blank. The page has been left blank intentionally. It is a terrific place to doodle or to make notes as you mull over what you just read.

Teacher Resources

The Complete Book of Activities, Games, Stories, Props, Recipes, and Dances by Pam Schiller and Jackie Silberg

The Giant Encyclopedia of Preschool Activities for Three-Year-Olds edited by Kathy Charner

The Giant Encyclopedia of Preschool Activities for Four-Year-Olds edited by Kathy Charner

A Survival Guide for Child Care Providers by Karen Levine

44 Routines That Make a Difference by the School Renaissance
Institute

The ABCs of Quality Child Care by Aida Maria Clark

All Eyes Up Here! by Tee Carr

The Busy Classroom by Patty Claycomb

*Challenging Behavior in Young Children: Understanding,
Preventing, and Responding Effectively* by Barbara Kaiser

*The Complete Book of Activities, Games, Stories, Props, Recipes,
and Dances* by Pam Schiller and Jackie Silberg

Conflict Resolution Activities That Work! by Kathleen M.
Hollenbeck

Cooking Art by MaryAnn F. Kohl and Jean Potter

Creating Child-Centered Classrooms edited by Pamela Coughlin

Creating Rooms of Wonder by Carol Seefeldt

Designs for Living and Learning by Deb Curtis and Margie Carter

Early Learning Environments That Work by Rebecca Isbell and
Betty Exelby

Fresh Approaches to Working With Problematic Behavior by
Adele M. Brodkin

The Giant Encyclopedia of Preschool Activities for Four-Year-Olds
edited by Kathy Charner

*The Giant Encyclopedia of Preschool Activities for Three-Year-
Olds* edited by Kathy Charner

Hard Facts on Smart Classroom Designs by Daniel Niemeyer

Hints From Heloise by Heloise

Kindness Curriculum by Judith Anne Rice

Kitchen Idea Bags by Sharon MacDonald

Life-Saving Strategies by Dottie Raymer

Making Toys for Infants and Toddlers by Linda G. Miller and Mary
Jo Gibbs

Making Toys for Preschool Children by Linda G. Miller and Mary
Jo Gibbs

Making Toys for School-Age Children by Linda G. Miller and
Mary Jo Gibbs

One Cup Cooking by Barbara Johnson and Betty Plemons

A Practical Guide to Quality Child Care by Pam Schiller and
    Patricia Carter Dyke

Practical Solutions to Practically Every Problem by Steffen Saifer

Skills for Preschool Teachers by Janice J. Beaty

Snacktivities! by MaryAnn F. Kohl and Jean Potter

A Survival Guide for Child Care Providers by Karen Levine

A Survival Guide for the Preschool Teacher by Jean Feldman

Teachable Transitions by Rae Pica

Teacher Made Materials That Really Teach by Judy Herr and
    Yvonne Libby Larson

Terrific Tips for Preschool Teachers by Barbara F. Backer

Terrific Transitions by Ellen Booth Church

There's Got to Be a Better Way by Becky Bailey

Transition Magician 2 by Mary Henthorne, Nola Larson, and Ruth
    Chvojicek

Transition Magician by Nola Larson, Mary Henthorne, and
    Barbara Plum

Transition Time by Jean Feldman

Transition Tips and Tricks by Jean Feldman

Wonderful Rooms Where Children Bloom by Jean Feldman

INDEX

SANITY SAVERS